W9-ANA-918

Schwartz/Silver

Cover Photograph:
MIT Rotch Library
Richard Mandelkorn

Chief Editor of Collection
Maurizio Vitta

Publishing Coordinator
Franca Rottola

Graphic Design
Studio CREA, Milano

Editing
Nick Dubrule

Translation
Aaron Maines

Colour Separation
Litofilms Italia, Bergamo

Printing
Puntografico, Brescia

First published
October 2001

ISBN 88-7838-088-1

Schwartz/Silver

Arguments for Building

Preface *by Robert H. Silver*
Essays *by Aaron Betsky*
and *Carlo Paganelli*

Contents

Preface

by Robert H. Silver, FAIA
Schwartz/Silver Architects

Looking back over the twenty-one years that Schwartz/Silver has been in practice, I am pleased that we have managed to resist one of the most prevalent fantasies of our profession: that of the "complete architect." It is a seductively authoritative idea which came from marrying the figure of the artist with that of the professional: the see-all, know-all genius. It's the kind of ideal that seemed appropriate to the age of Palladio, or even H. H. Richardson, but it's awkward and ill-suited to the present. Most architecture is no longer defined by the simple need to address the aspirations of a single over-arching patron, now it is beholden to a multiplicity of constituencies, regulations and guidelines, let alone the encroaching demands of a far more densely developed social and physical context. A host of specialist expertise is needed, and projects have developed complexities that are unrealistic for a single human brain to handle.

When Warren Schwartz and I started working together at other firms during the 1970s, we were a little embarrassed to discover that each of us was more productive working with the other than we were alone. It was perhaps embarrassing to our colleagues as well. They came up with nicknames for us: Warren was "the Pencil" and I was "the Eraser." But the fact was that the projects we designed were successful: we made an inventive team. The personal qualities that may have been a weakness working individually became a strength working together. And so, paradoxically, our sense of incompleteness became a driving force for the firm we founded together. As it grew, it was no longer just about our personalities and predilections, but those of an engagingly creative group of diverse individuals that are excited by working together. Our colleagues help supplement our partial insights with their partial insights. For everyone, it is much more gratifying to be involved in design as a participant than be relegated to a pawn in somebody else's game.

By working together, we strive to find that sense of completion vested in the traditional ideal. Of course, even with the heterogeneity of age and experience collected in our office, it is a completion that is still unfulfilled. We can only know our way around a building design the way any architect does. The insights of users, clients, neighbors and other non-architects are just as necessary to the fulfillment of our desire for a totally assured design. Each project presents a new opportunity to discover the physical resolution of the program in the community of interests we draw together. It requires the kind of collaboration that makes design relevant and responsive. The actual outcome is always unpredictable and different. It is an adventure — given definition by the particular circumstances of the project rather than any controlling need for consistency in our office portfolio.

So, looking forward, I am pleased to find that our personal failure to fit the mold of "complete architect" has spawned qualities to make our practice, in the complex and constrained world in which we find ourselves, that much more rewarding and engaging.

Arguments for Building

by Aaron Betsky

Born out of postmodern formal and social concerns[1], the firm of Schwartz/Silver Architects has developed into an argumentative collection of bricoleurs[2], scavenging through the fertile fields of architecture. Out of what they collect, they make moments of civic order within the confusion of the modern American city. Confined by neither style nor a standard approach to their commissions, the firm sees itself as making "propositions in built form." Varying from arguments for civic dignity to celebrations of a community's cultural assets, and from the careful renovation of existing conditions to the establishment of openings towards new form, their work is varied. Yet it is almost always up to the task at hand.

The firm defines its work in two ways. The first is to place itself within its local context while adopting and adapting more generally accepted forms and methods. They share this approach with many other medium-sized American firms who focus on what the profession calls "design" (as opposed to production or some other form of facilitating construction). They understand themselves as a Boston firm, working within local styles and methods of construction. In their work, they seek to find new ways of developing these traditions, without losing the logic or beauty that these ways of doing things bring with them. At the same time, Schwartz/Silver has the same place in the culture industry as any other firm of its size and intentions, and must make a place for its buildings within an increasingly global culture. Not only is the firm now working far outside its native area, but its forms and strategies share as much with firms in other parts of the world as they do with its local counterparts. The result is a kind of "glocal" mix of elements.

As a philosophical basis to understand and interpret their work and its challenges, Schwartz/Silver has turned to the writings of the Russian literary critic Mikhail Bakhtin. Adapting his writings about novels, they adopt his belief that their art exists in and strengthens the essential dialogue out of which we make our shared culture: "Only dialogue reveals potentials. It does so by addressing them, by provoking a specific answer that actualizes the potential, albeit in a particular or incomplete way. At the same time, the questioner necessarily undergoes the same process, which helps him comprehend unsuspected potentials in his own culture."[3] The result of this give-and-take is an "elastic environment of other, alien words about the same object... It is precisely in the process of living interaction with this specific environment that the word may be individualized and given stylistic shape."[4]

This pluralistic environment, in which the work, the maker and the audience are continually engaged in a kind of cultural negotiation out of which shared structures of cognition and empathy arise, is an almost perfect definition of the sort of Postmodernism popularized by critics from Charles Jencks[5] to Kenneth Frampton.[6] What sets Schwartz/Silver apart is their recognition of the "obscuring mist of mixed metaphors upon mixed metaphors"[7] that never resolve into one particular form of address. The result is not a collection of direct signs, but a carefully blended set of references that are rarely direct.

This sense of indirection is increased by the firm's modernist tendencies towards both abstraction and functional and structural expression. As a result of the literal translation of how the building is made, how it is used, and how building materials and compositions are, for both cultural and economic reasons more generic (or "normative," as Frampton would put it), their buildings have a high degree of abstraction. At the same time, the work becomes, perhaps only because of the translation of the theory from language to architecture, but also because of the firm's own approach, more densely layered with colluding and colliding metaphors. Yet these references all exist on the level of a surface or sign, and rarely inflect spatial arrangements that are generated from functional or contextual needs.

This is perhaps only fitting. Unlike in the novel, in which the protagonist to which the reader transfers her or his sympathies is fictional, in this case the characters are other library users, students, aquarium visitors or plaintiffs in a courtroom. The architects can only achieve their results by generalizing or abstracting the characteristics of such users, and thus they have recourse to the general methods architecture has at hand to accomplish this: the creation of shared spaces, the development of common responses to gravity, light and materials, and references to a commonly understood civic language. Empathy in architecture is usually achieved through such ends. Schwartz/Silver is careful to emphasize the specificity and incompleteness of its task, thus saving it from the contradictions inherent in grand narrative strategies. What Schwartz/Silver contributes to the arrangement of spaces and forms we inhabit is a kind of "supplement" (an idea also picked up by the likes of Jacques Derrida[8]) that is integral to and indistinguishable from the actual built environment. What it allows for is a form of essential empathy through which the viewer or user can connect with other users of the same structures. Though their approach is not by any means unique, each of their buildings thus does gain by being rooted in its place and task.

The development of this architecture has its roots in the partners' training. Warren Schwartz arrived in Boston after training at Cornell University in the early 1960s to attend Harvard's Graduate School of Design. Robert Silver attended the same graduate program after obtaining undergraduate degrees in physics at Queens College in New York and architecture at Cambridge University in England. What they shared was an inculcation in an architectural culture that sought to base its assumptions on (real or imagined) scientific theories. The sciences themselves, however, were tending towards the collage of perspective necessary in a post-quantum era. The sciences had also, since at least the early 1930s, been shifting their focus towards the social arena. The kind of architecture which Schwartz and Silver learned, and in which they began to practice, was part and parcel of the mechanisms

Right, East Cambridge Savings Bank. Far right, Wellesley Fire Station.

PHOTO: STEVE ROSENTHAL

PHOTO: MICK HALES

of social engineering that bloomed into the experiments of the Great Society and the tragedies of the Vietnam War.

The equivalent of such programs in the Boston architectural scene were the redevelopment projects undertaken under the leadership of the urban planner Edward Logue. By inflecting the scorched earth tactics of the 1950s that replaced urban fabric with abstract elements of what would turn out to be a failed utopia, towards the preservation of existing neighborhoods and architectural forms, Logue brought notions of collage, multiple perspectives (though still governed by shared and often imposed principles) and social narrative into urban planning practices.[9]

Working first for the Boston Redevelopment Authority, and then for one of its principal architects, Charles Hilgenhurst, Schwartz and Silver had a direct role in many of Logue's projects. It was only after Hilgenhurst's untimely death in 1980 that they moved resolutely out of the realm of planning, on which so much of architecture's attention was focused in the late 1960s and early 1970s, to the making of small buildings. They point to a building they worked on while still in Hilgenhurst's office, the East Cambridge Savings Bank of 1979, as the generator of much of their later work.

The bank is an early effort to combine contextual planning with the insertion of modern elements. While respecting the existing banking hall, the new addition curves away from the street's building line to enclose a space that serves semi-public circulation. The new is highly functional and discreet, stating its purpose while respecting the situation in which it finds itself. It is a clear translation of the small bank's position as an institution, that seeks both to impress and to renovate its neighborhood. As such, the design has a remarkable similarity to the thoughtful collages proposed by James Stirling at the time for projects such as the Derby (United Kingdom) Civic Center (1970).

The firm combined a background in planning with then fashionable notions of historical reference that treated all architectural elements as pieces in a linguistic system. Adopting and adapting signifiers, the firm made direct references to the context, the building type which they were addressing, or the system of building materials they were using to construct their buildings. Perhaps the best example of such an approach is their Wellesley Fire Station of 1984-87. Here they designed a civic focal point that inhabitants can recognize as a fire station, both because of its references to existing buildings of this type and because of its frank exposition of functional elements.

Schwartz/Silver showed themselves to be the best kinds of Postmodernists: the sort who can compose buildings that seek to be legible to a multitude of viewers and users while exposing how and why they are made, all shaped together into a package that makes these different source points come together into a modern monument.

What Schwartz/Silver was adding to its planning approach was a cloak of elements that were abstractions of structure, traditional building methods and the catalog of pieces generated by economic logic, that make up the modernist vocabulary. Made possible by the freedom from doctrine Postmodernism gave architects, it served to humanize and localize their work. It also created a problem for them which they still have not solved: though it made them flexible enough to address almost any commission that comes their way with skill and even bravura, the resulting heterogeneity of their work makes it difficult to define, and thus "sell," the firm.

Schwartz/Silver's early work of careful additions and small inventions came to an end with two projects in 1985: Warren Schwartz's weekend house in Tanglewood and their collaboration with Frank Gehry on the Tower Records project. With the latter, they began to explore a form of call-and-response with existing conditions, program and building methods that did not so much imitate or adapt those constituent elements, as form them into a coherent and confident new shape. With the former, Schwartz reached back to a shared architectural history to make new forms. While quoting Scamozzi's Villa Pisani (1576), the Tanglewood house is too abstract and plays too many games with symmetry to be immediately recognizable as a historic artifact.

The mid-1980s also brought the addition of Bob Miklos to the firm as a principal, and his arrival coincided with the firm's greater expression of building structure. The expository use of wood or steel frames came to serve as a skeleton on which the firm could erect its newly coalescing forms. While in the Proctor Academy of 1992-95 the wood

PHOTO: CHRIS LITTLE

PHOTO: DAVID HEWITT

Far left, the House at Tanglewood. Left, 360 Newbury St. (Tower Records).

frame resembles a thinned-out and attenuated barn the community has raised to shelter learning, in the MIT Rotch Library project (1988-91) it is a bravura exposition of the complex steel structure necessary to hollow out space in an extremely compacted and impacted sliver of building, and in the Two Rivers Landing Museum Complex (1994-96) it becomes a decorative texture that adds elegance to its drab and economically depressed setting.

Schwartz/Silver's work of the last decade has in this manner developed a strong structure. It also presents a series of clearly articulated forms. What they have lately managed to create within this framework is a set of beautiful spaces. These range from the highly personal and expressive interstitial spaces they carved out of the Davoli-McDonagh House (1999-) for clients who wanted a house that would "express movement," to the formal elegance of the reading room at the Hyde Park Branch Library (1996-2000). They also include the pared-down main courtroom at the Chelsea Trial Court (1992-2000) and the auditorium at the Newburyport Firehouse Arts Center (1988-91).

What distinguishes these recent buildings is the complex and subtle relationships they establish between these spaces and the outsides, as well as the increasing complexity of the forms themselves. Schwartz/Silver has always been fond of slipping things over and through each other, as they do with the side wall of the Farnsworth Art Museum (1997-1998) or the addition of the Hyde Park Library. In recent buildings, this method of collage has become conceptual as well as actual. It serves to dematerialize their buildings and intensify them at the same time. A good example would be the proposed Admissions Building for St. John's University in New York (1999-), which is currently waiting for funding. Here the whole building seems to be slipping off its base, which is a strong, stone affair that holds the building to its sloping site. Rendered in a manner that is reminiscent of both the Nordic classicism of Gunnar Asplund and the spare, brick modernism common to institutional buildings of the 1950s, the structure makes a virtue of the subtle ways in which it can appear humble and completely contingent. Then the public spaces at the building's East end burst out from under these restraints, gesturing out to both the students (and prospective students) they serve and the Cesar Pelli-designed chapel adjacent to the site.

While almost all of Schwartz/Silver's buildings deploy such strategies of implosion, intensification and slippage, one can start to see certain themes develop across the work. There is the structural expressionism already mentioned above, which keeps coming up as way of tying complex elements together. Then there remains the use of the "vernacular" or local building elements, as in Newburyport or at the Proctor Academy. The primacy of the central space and the wrapping of that space with an appropriate, but wholly modern, shape is the harbinger of projects such as the Hyde Park Library. These are all continuations of the firm's earlier concerns.

Two new approaches have joined their palette. One delves even deeper into the nature of the commission. In some cases, as in the proposed addition to the Ames Free Library, this excavation is literal. It is a way of making the new in a realm that is free to establish itself as such, while still being respectful of existing conditions. Here the firm is making some of their most radically new forms by exploring construction. From its roots in the hidden addition to the MIT Library, to the cave of Ames, this architecture is becoming more and more pared-down and abstract. Rooted in the simple addition and reorganization the firm designed for the Bowdoin College Museum of Art in 1999, it is an approach that comes close to being no more and no less than a manipulation of the landscape. In a sense, this is the ultimate form of contextualism, as the building disappears quite literally into the "ground." Yet Schwartz/Silver is able to mine even this self-masking territory to great effect. This is true both formally, as the splayed plans begin to articulate a relationship between Henry Hobson Richardson's strong box and the contours of the landscape, and in terms of the user's experience, as the design leads one on carefully calibrated paths towards beautifully sheltered rooms.

The other approach explodes out from the existing conditions. This kind of exuberance appears to be quite new in the firm's history, and is perhaps influenced by the current interest of architects in general in such expressive shapes. Certainly the New England Aquarium entrance (and the proposed renovation of the whole building) of 1994-98 bears a certain resemblance to the work not only of Frank Gehry, but also of Zaha Hadid of London and Coop Himmelb(l)au of Vienna. Like this work, the Aquarium has the sense of existing as a set of unstable plates colliding to form a structure that is not quite coherent, but centripetal. One is sucked into a shared experience by an architecture whose multitude of references, as well as its strong figural presence, catch one's attention.

Certainly such an approach makes sense given the Aquarium's nature as a tourist attraction that must sign itself at the edge of a cluster of highrises. It serves to bring in the crowds, both literally and metaphorically. Somehow the addition also becomes a metaphor for a ship, a whale or any number of other marine occurrences. Language here becomes a slippery thing that manages to speak in the forked tongue of a generic cultural attractor and a site-specific building at the same time. This implosive approach then becomes the logical methodology for the design of the nearby Institute of Contemporary Art. Schwartz/Silver has proposed a new building for this institution on the as-of-yet undeveloped area of Boston's Fan Pier. In their design the folded plates open the public spaces up to the spectacular views across the harbor and make the small building look much larger. They also serve as a metaphor for the unstable relationship contemporary art has to its surroundings.

The continuity of a concern for metaphoric dialogue, structural and functional expression, linguistic expression, and collage design are thus finding new forms in the firm's work. These shapes are as much part of the current architectural culture as they are a response to the Schwartz/Silver's own internal development, and for the members of the firm that is not a negative comment. They see themselves as continually in dialogue not only among themselves and with their clients or users, but also with the culture of which they are part.[10]

The most recent expression of this openness can be glimpsed in their proposal for the Louisiana State University Museum of Art in Baton Rouge. Here they are once again adapting and adopting forms from elsewhere, such as Renzo Piano's design for the Menil Collection in Texas (1986). They combine his parallel galleries shaded by a louvered roof with references to such a variety of southern types as the colonnaded mansions of the Louisiana Plantations, to the "Dog Trot" houses, to Louis Kahn's Kimbell Art Museum of 1971, to create an elegant and grand monument. Their sources come out of a response to climate and the need to symbolize culture, and thus the form seems appropriate. It also serves to give this nascent institution a sense of itself that can stand up against its sprawling surroundings and anchor this suburban place. As such, the Baton Rouge building serves as a counterpoint to the battlements of the Chelsea Trial Court, which manages to create the same kind of larger-than-life clarity and inner serenity in a surrounding that is almost exactly the opposite to that of the LSU Museum of Art.

The question still remains whether there is something singular that identifies the work of Schwartz/Silver. They are not tending towards any particular style or definable set of forms. Certainly each of their buildings is a specific response to a given set of conditions. It is also clear that they enjoy letting their architecture speak whatever language is in currency, whether within the neighborhood they build, the typological history in which the commission finds itself, or the community of designers and other cultural producers then operating. They are not architects who impose an unvarying style on their work. They still see themselves working in dialogue with all those conditions in which they work. The result may not be an architecture that one can easily identify. It is instead a set of carefully reasoned arguments for an architecture that uses its means to state a shared set of experiences, memories and expectations in a specific location at a particular time. Given the humble beauty of their buildings, this is more than enough.

Aaron Betsky is Director of the Netherlands Architecture Institute.

Notes

1 I use "postmodern" here not so much in the popular sense of the term, but as the rediscovery of social narrative inherent in forms produced with modern technology. See Peter Bürger, *Theory of the Avant-Garde*, tr. by Michael Shaw (Minneapolis: University of Minneapolis Press, 1985) or Pierre Bourdieu, *The Field of Cultural Production*, ed. by Randal Johnson (New York: Columbia University Press, 1993)

2 As defined by Claude Lévi-Strauss in *The Savage Mind* (Chicago: University of Chicago Press, 1966)

3 Gary Saul Morson, Caryl Emerson, *Mikhail Bakhtin: Creation of a Prosaics* (Stanford: Stanford University Press, 1990), p. 56.

4 Ibid, p. 50.

5 Charles Jencks, *The Language of Postmodern Architecture* (New York: Rizzoli International Publications, 1977)

6 Kenneth Frampton, *Studies in Tectonic Culture: The Poetics of Construction in Nineteenth and Twentieth Century Architecture* (Cambridge, MA: The MIT Press, 1995).

7 Morson, p. 54.

8 For the best summation of Derrida's theories seen from an art historical perspective, see: Gregory Ulmer, "The Object of Post-Criticism," in Hal Foster, *The Anti-Aesthetic: Essays on Postmodern Culture* (Port Townsend, WA: Bay Press, 1983), pp. 83-110

9 See Edward Logue, David Crane, John F. Collins, Mayor, et al. 1965-75 *General Plan for the City of Boston and the Regional Core.*

10 Conversation with Warren Schwartz, Robert Silver, April 22, 2000

Form and Regeneration

by Carlo Paganelli

Metamorphosis and Identity

The dynamism of the American spirit, the diffuse modularity of the inhabited constructions and the speed of constructive systems are at the base of frequent transformations of the American urban landscape. Nevertheless, in the face of continuous radical mutations – assisted by an economic system that establishes the costs and revenue of a construction based on a specific timeframe and subject to external market forces – there also exists the activity of significant restructuring and readaptation of existing structures. And it is in this sensitive building sector that the architecture studio of Schwartz/Silver Architects, with its headquarters in Boston, concentrates its efforts. An effort to superimpose one structure on another, while attempting to preserve the original memory and concept, is at the heart of every intervention this Boston studio undertakes. The memory of an architecture, and therefore of a place, represents a tangible sign of the passing of time. The sedimentation of interventions underlines, in the most concrete and visible forms, the mutations of the activities that have followed one another over time, tracing a kind of historical text. It is a sociocultural text mediated through the language of architecture – a non-verbal, non-written language that is nevertheless dense with symbols.

The American urban scene is basically articulated by two opposing polarities. On one side, there is the complete destruction of the preexisting, carried out in order to create new opportunities. On the other, the continuous work of stitching, which blends the new with the old, generating hybrid and complex architectures that unexpectedly reveal cultural continuity with an urban phenomenon of European origins. The most significant datum is that even though the memories of the past are evident, the contemporary American city emerges with extraordinary evocative force in all its originality, aggressiveness and unity. In just this sense Vincent Scully vindicated the style in a passage of his book *American Architecture and Urbanism* (New York 1969): "This urban scene is an authentically American product...It is our most complete work of art, multiform and terrible. Its unity, its inconceivable brutality, even its pure visual magnificence can never be denied."

Respect for the site versus magnificence of style

Even if they are not against every formal emphasis – as indicated by the term versus – the interventions undertaken by Schwartz/Silver demonstrate more than anything else a profound respect for the preexisting structure. The project for the expansion of the Cornell University Library, in Ithaca, New York, is a striking example of respect for the site and its architectural history. It is a respect that does not, however, renounce delicate signs of modernity, destined to fix the intervention's moment in time. Characterized by a blending together with a classical construction, the addition of a new organism to the central body of Cornell University could have been a difficult operation of architectural transplantation, most likely destined to provoke clamorous commentary. The decision to create a forward body with an ample glass surface enabled the architects to bypass any stylistic backlash, realizing the double goal of dematerializing the new structure as much as possible and, simultaneously, highlighting the grand neoclassic-style cupola at the edifice's apex. This way an ideal magnifying lens was placed under the cupola, emphasizing its harmonious proportions. The new library plays with mirrored images like a giant, resplendent crystal. By day it reflects its surroundings, organically inserting itself in the site. At night it projects its own internal spaces out to the campus by means of an attentively managed technical illumination, inverting the perception of the architecture from volume to concave body.

Regeneration versus destruction

In this case versus should be interpreted in its fullest significance of programmatic opposition. The acceptance of an architecture generated by other architectures, like that realized by Schwartz/Silver, may be an unusual route for the vast majority of American architects. Schwartz/Silver Architects seem to place themselves in a position quite distant from the general tendency. Essentially, they seem to wish to take refuge in the aristocratic niche of the cultured and out-of-the-ordinary minority. In reality, this is a behavior of constructive criticism towards the pragmatic American spirit, which, especially in the world of architecture, seems in harmony with those who believe that modernity and progress can only be created from a *tabula rasa*. Traces of this radical spirit can also be found in personalities far from the architectural world – for example in a nineteenth-century writer like Nathaniel Hawthorne. In his book *The Marble Faun*, written in 1860, he launched rather explicit extremist messages like: "Every city must be capable of purifying itself, with fire and progressive ruin, at least once every half a century."

But above and beyond the programmed destruction invoked by writers and thinkers, some American cities were truly generated by actual disasters, which in some way or another conditioned their destiny and development. It is also important to remember that American contemporary imagination is awash with the dramatic beauty of catastrophes – highways disintegrated by earthquakes, skyscrapers in flames, disastrous nuclear explosions, and metropolitan areas stalked by criminal gangs – all examples of prime Hollywood cinematic material. Metropolitan nightmares take shape in a cinema in which the fragility of the new and the degradation of the past suggest the ghosts of ruin, even if shielded by current economic prosperity. The image of imminent destruction winds its way through even the most unexpected mediums, like comics, and even in those destined for the youngest readers. In Walt Disney comic strips, the fire hydrant is a dramatic icon, a constant presence in the urban landscape, a sign that reminds the reader of the risk of fire in the city. Suburban houses, built entirely of wood, burn intensely and often. It is a common conviction that, sooner or later, fire will destroy some habitation, especially houses that have been abandoned or are sparsely inhabited. This contributes an element of "natural" change to the urban scene. The language that reminds us of an architecture which trembles is not only a poetic *transfert*; it is a creative tension linked to reality. Even if Europe is not immune to this language, it must be underlined that it is born of diverse motivations compared to the United States. Several years ago, for the Architectural Biennale in Venice, Arata Isozaki dedicated the entire Japanese pavilion – of which he was commissary – to the earthquake that had devastated the city of Kobe, a small urban center near Osaka. The so-called "fractured" architecture undoubtedly represents a world rife with uncertainties and anxieties – from ecological disasters to the population explosion – but with its surprising and unexpected forms it feeds new scientific and epistemological paradigms. When this particular language does not remain on the surface as simple formal differentiation it performs as an exorcising function more than as a portrait of reality. The thin titanium layers of the Gehry's Guggenheim Museum in Bilbao, the fractured steel cuts of the Jewish Museum in Berlin designed by Libeskind, or the Spittelau Viaduct in Vienna by Zaha Hadid, similar in appearance to a railway disaster, in all their dramatic beauty truly seem the long and threatening shadows of a century that is finishing. The origins of "fractured" architecture, of the symbolic apparatus, disobedient and Dionysian, is contrary to the Apollonian serenity of structural symmetry. This left its first traces in Jakob Hittorf's work, representing the unexpected polychromy of Classical temples. At the time – we're talking about a period stretching between the first and second half of the 1800's – these were considered transgressive and rather unorthodox.

A small, planned catastrophe

Two Rivers Landing is a new structure created by Schwartz/Silver in which one can identify veiled traces of the "ruinist" poetry present in the collective subconscious of American architects. The intervention in question, designed to house the National Canal Museum and the Crayola Factory Museum, is characterized by a primarily steel and glass construction. The new structure is strongly contrasted with a rigorous orthogonal scansion which suggests the image of industrial archeology. The "transgression" is inserted in a point of passage between two preexisting factory structures through a slightly inclined walkway, one that in any case interrupts the cold orthogonal order of the composition. The configuration of this additional construction insinuates the idea of a kind of small telluric shock which, even if it hasn't provoked great damage, has nevertheless left a dramatic sign of its passage in the anomalous inclination of the structure. Two Rivers Landing is a little bit of transgression, a little bit of veiled citation to the ruinism of certain of James Stirling's creations from the 1980's, and it is undoubtedly one of the most creative interventions produced by Schwartz/Silver.

The value of origins

The expansion of the Boston Athenaeum is one of the more demanding renovation interventions taken on by Schwartz/Silver, and it is the most emblematic of philological rigor and adherence to a theme. A prestigious institution founded in 1807, the Boston Athenaeum is known throughout the United States not only for its vast collection of texts and works of art, but also because it conserves all the volumes of George Washington's private library. The renovation project primarily dealt with functional reorganization and the construction of several furnishing elements that included catwalks and specialized equipment destined for the reading public and visitors who come to view the art collections. Well aware of the ramifications of an intervention in a structure of such important historical value for the United States and, above all, the city of Boston, Schwartz/Silver aimed for a kind of in-depth reading of the contrast between history and modernity. Architecture as a container for atemporality was the guideline for creating spaces with a double value, capable of hosting traditional forms as well as new solutions. The intervention in an historical organism of considerable symbolic value like the Boston Athenaeum brought up a series of methodological considerations including, for example, the tension between present and past, as well as the tension between present and future. Both are reflections that characterize the dynamic aspect of the life of an edifice. In this direction, Schwartz/Silver Architect's projectural philosophy can be traced to Ruskin's theories. In essence, the edifice is comparable to a biological organism in so far as no entity belonging to this universe is a stranger to the laws of life. Once the fact that even architecture is inserted in the harmony of nature has been established, it is natural that it should be considered as a living organism. The harmony that Ruskin is referring to does not belong to a static order, removed from time, but rather is inserted in a dynamic context in which all the elements relate to one another. Essentially, an architecture must be designed with an eye cast to its possible and potential developments over the entire span of its long life.

Coherence towards architectural manufacture

In Schwartz/Silver's vision, the edifice is an organism whose natural authenticity must not be betrayed. An expansion or renovation undertaken without a proper consideration of a building's condition is considered a morally incorrect action. In the Schwartzian vision, the edifice is not simply a designed entity, and much less an element generated by architectural thought, but rather a concrete presence with its own body. Its solid physical presence is the result of a projectural idea transformed into the material - into a physical entity. This critical assertion that underlines every intervention is part of the metaprojectural context of every work realized. The architecture that is to be worked with is deeply and thoughtfully analyzed in order to verify how it has inserted itself in the natural as well as the urban context. Examining the relationships between edifice and historical context supplies a projectural map that is capable of providing information helpful for the creation of an intervention aligned with the modern concept of conservation of the historical-architectural patrimony.

The expansion of the New England Aquarium in Boston appears to be a whole different kettle of fish. The subject and realization of this recent intervention appear to be rather unusual compared to the normal client requests that Schwartz/Silver must satisfy. (Usually they are committed to the delicate coupling of new architectural organisms with structures that are historical, or in any case, far from contemporary). The theme was to revitalize and give a new image to an edifice of no particular significance, constructed some twenty years ago. The expansion is essentially an addition destined for the aquarium's western entrance. The strong formal characterization of the New England Aquarium follows an unusual logic, though one that is somewhat in fashion among many groups of architects, not just in the United States but also in Europe and Asia. The extreme creative liberty that characterizes the world of contemporary architecture has breathed life into a remarkably interesting phenomenon. It has prompted a radical inversion of the urban project's formative phase. The city and the metropolis are no longer simply generators of the cornerstone upon which an architecture based on preliminary plans is founded (an architecture destined to supply a functional and morphological framework that can be built upon), now it is the selfsame architecture which interprets an urban role capable of giving identity to the metropolis. The aquarium, its pointed forms extended towards the ocean almost suggesting a terrestrial extension into the marine world, is a colonizing element of the site. The strong semantic seduction launched into both its surroundings and to the entire city constitutes the sense of an urbanism overturned. Moving above and beyond every mediation, the architecture's language has appropriated the urban dimension in its most intrinsic extension. Therefore the architecture loses that subordinate status usually conferred upon it with respect to the urban fabric, through the amplification of its own composite identity. This is no simple, small-scale mutation, but one that will in the long run undoubtedly create new disciplinary redefinitions. In the meantime, in more than one forum there is already talk of eliminating historical-critical definitions which have been considered immutable, like "city architecture," "for the city," or "in the city," and substituting them with the neologism "architecture/city." This inversion of tendency stems from a variety of motivational factors. Among many, one clear example is the group of architects who see the city today in a moment of profound mutation through a kind of ideal miniaturization. The strong and growing complexity of individual and collective behavior that marks the variegated geography of the metropolitan territories induces a sort of miniaturization of the urban space that vindicates the semantic value. Seen through the lens of architecture, the city seems to implode and condense into a space that can be referred to as a dense, concentrated imagination – one that is limited but absolute.

The city as iconic nucleus subtracted from the historical workability expressed by the urbanistic

On the contemporary scene there is an increasingly evident architecture with an identity that is very close to that of "intelligent" urban structure. It is a composition that can be interrogated like a kind of oracle which, even if hermetic, is in any case capable of initiating a dialogue with its surroundings, and with metropolitan man. It is an architecture anxiously replete with strong suggestions like those generated by the media and by the new interactive communication technologies. In accepted projectural practices the dense and polarized architecture is slowly but surely replacing the city of traces, of urban textures, of divisions between public and private spaces. The "loose" city in new and old centralities is being configured as a visual emblem rich in symbols and signs. In this context marked by "individualistic architecture" even the statutes of time and place mutate. Contrary to just a few years ago, the dilated time of the urbanistic is now oriented towards the much more restricted time of architecture. It is precisely because of this temporal mutation that the single architecture is disseminated in the form of motes and atoms that are different from one another, until they culminate in a dense stain constituted by a plurality of individual elements separable by form and vocation. In the case of the New England Aquarium, its evocative force as connective machine between earth and sea explains how roadway traces and urban textures, spaces and sites, as well as environments and contexts, are all absorbed in architectural manufacture in the form of memory, an element at the base of its configuration and architectural composition.

Architecture as simulacrum

Essentially, hypotheses advanced years ago when architecture was defined as a mass medium with its own communicational language are now becoming concrete realities. The dense language of contemporary architecture generates edifices which, reacting on a subliminal level, behave like simulacrums constituted by stratifications of thresholds and urban temporality. These are capable of substituting for any given urbanistic plan, thereby enunciating a sort of *forma urbis* that has been reexamined and corrected. Naturally, this is a mobile *forma urbis*, one that is dynamic and characterized by its own autonomy, and can be interpreted as a participating element in the nature of the symbol, as the ideogram of a language that is in the process of being formed and therefore open to improvement.

Carlo Paganelli is a journalist and architecture critic based in Milan.

Works

The Rotch Library

Massachusetts Institute of Technology, Cambridge, MA
1988-1991

The Library of Art, Architecture and Planning is one of the Massachusetts Institute of Technology's five divisional libraries. Housing the second largest collection of architectural documents in the United States, the library serves as an important research center for both the Institute and the architectural community.

Plans for the library expansion were many years in the making but had been abandoned after several architects failed to solve the issues of the long and narrow site. The program required an addition of about 2,000 square meters to the existing 850 square meter library. The extreme narrowness of the space available for the addition was also limited in its vertical dimension. It could not exceed the height of the historic domed building to which the addition would be joined, and the bottom had to be six meters above ground to allow clearance for an essential service yard underneath. Within these restrictions, the required building area could only be achieved by creating six levels, with the floor slabs only twenty centimeters thick and 2-1/2 meters apart.

Schwartz/Silver's design solution is based in an unusual technical innovation: to make the floors structurally sound, they are suspended from massive roof girders, with frequent hangers hidden between the stacks. The weight of the books is carried from above, eliminating beams in the floors, and making such thin floor slabs feasible. Then, to provide easy turning space for vehicles in the service yard below, structural columns are placed only along the perimeter, pairs of which are parted so that trucks can easily enter and exit. Separating the addition from the original structure is a 1-1/2 meter wide slot spanning the width of building. This allows the new and old buildings to stand independently, meet seismic code requirements, and preserve the original 1930s facade as an architectural artifact. The slot also allows skylights to replace natural light that would otherwise have been blocked by the addition.

The unusual parameters of the project, and its design response, have made the Rotch Library a frequent study project for architecture students and librarians, as well as a popular workspace for MIT students.

Client:
Massachusetts Institute of Technology
Structural Engineer:
Simpson Gumpertz & Heger Inc.
MEP Engineer:
R. G. Vanderweil Engineers
Contractor:
George B.H. Macomber Company
Photographer:
Chuck Choi
Schwartz/Silver Project Team:
Warren Schwartz
Robert Silver
Ann Pitt
Laura Briggs
Randolph Meiklejohn
Chris Downey
Elise Gispan
Nancy Hackett

Opposite page, partial view of Rotch Library (Building 7A) from between Buildings 11 and 13. Left, the site before construction, marked to test vehicular accessibility.

Levels 4, 5 & 6.

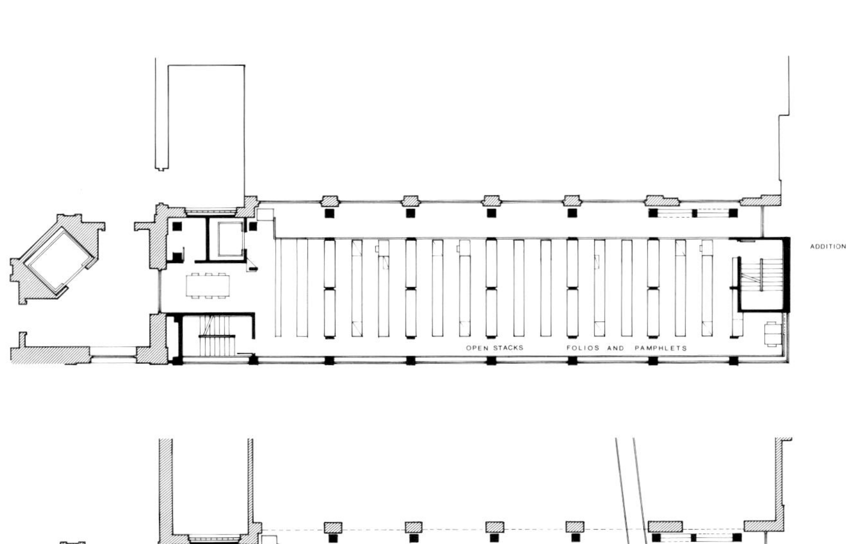

Level 3.

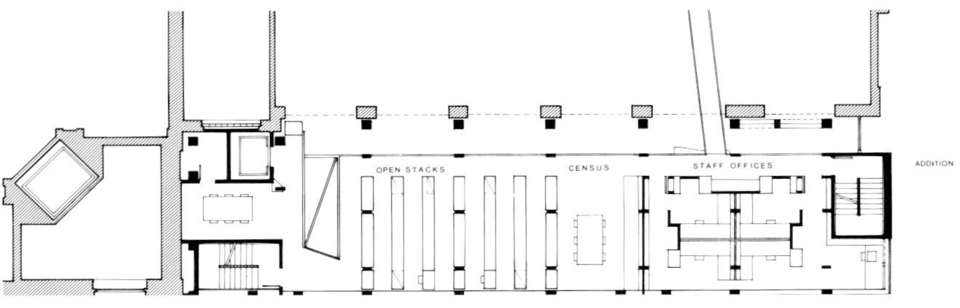

Level 2.

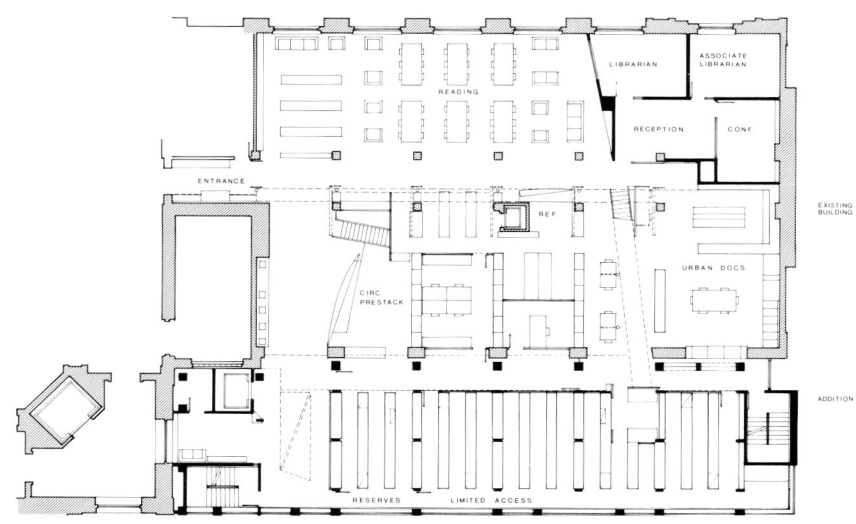

Level 1.

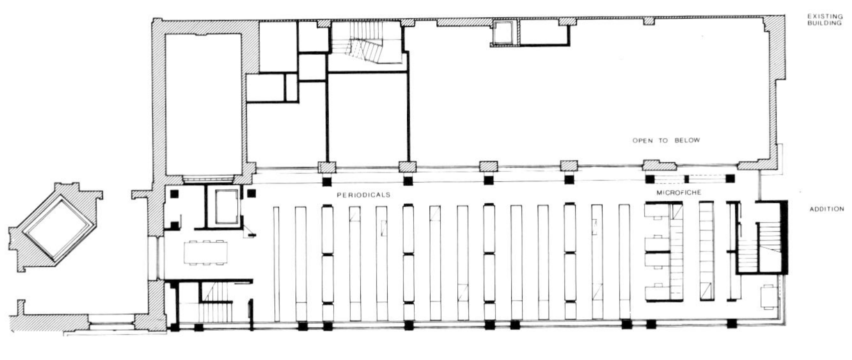

Level 0.

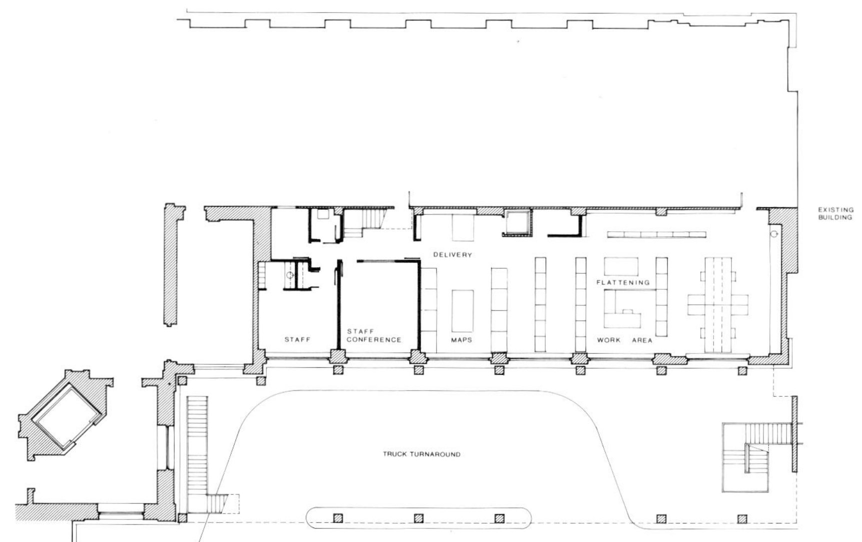

Axonometric diagram of building context.

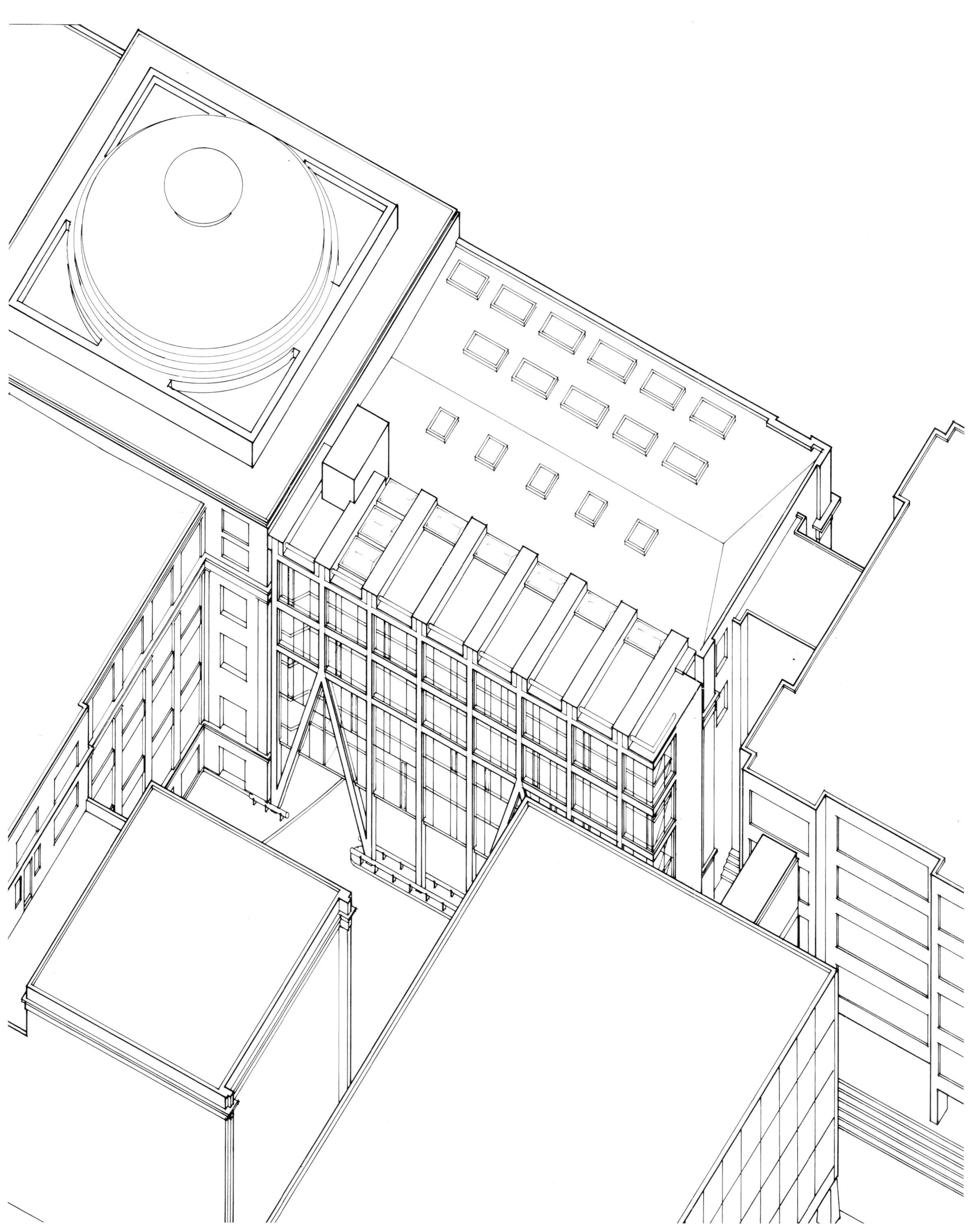

View of Rotch
Library addition
from Building 11.

View of Rotch Library addition from over roadway between Buildings 9 and 13.

View of
Rotch Library
addition facade.

View of fourth and fifth levels of the addition from the architecture studios on the third floor of the main building (Building 7).

Below, balconies overlooking the open slot between the main building and the floors in the addition.
Bottom, exposed structural systems in the addition.

Below, the circulation desk in the main building, leading into the addition.
Bottom, open spaces adjoining book stacks.

The Firehouse Arts Center

Newburyport, MA, 1988-1991

In a major effort to preserve the Federal buildings of its downtown, against a tide of development in the late 1960s and early 1970s, the City of Newburyport succeeded in creating a spectacular visitor attraction from its architecture, which has proven fertile ground for small shops and restaurants. To give a civic focus to the district, and under pressure from local arts groups, the City identified a disused firehouse to be converted into a center for performing and visual arts. This was an interesting reversion towards its original purpose: before its use as a firehouse beginning in 1864, the building had been a Lyceum where Daniel Webster and Ralph Waldo Emerson had given public lectures. The program for the new arts facility called for a 200-seat, fully equipped, professional theater, together with an art gallery and a café.

The challenge was how to effect such a dramatic change of use for the building and provide additional space, while at the same time respecting its history and the laudable work of the preservationists on the entire district. Schwartz/Silver's solution was to design an addition which was modern enough not to undermine the integrity of the original building by false imitation, and yet sympathetic enough to the architectural heritage of the city to be a part of it. The addition achieves this balance by establishing itself as a second front to the building, although it is situated at the back. Visible from the waterfront and the north bank of the river, it gives prominence to the arts center and also acts as a landmark for the city. The original facade on Market Square was returned to its late nineteenth century appearance, manifesting the evolution of the building from lyceum to firehouse to arts center as an integral part of its identity.

Client:
City of Newburyport
Structural Engineer:
LeMessurier Consultants
MEP Engineer:
Fitzemeyer & Tocci, Inc.
Theater Consultant:
Theatre Projects Consultants Inc.
Contractors:
Castagna Construction Corp. (Phase I)
P & H General Contractors Inc. (Phase II)
Photographer:
Jeff Goldberg/Esto
Schwartz/Silver Project Team:
Robert Miklos
Randolph Meiklejohn
Rania Matar
Elise Gispan
David Stern
James McQueen

Opposite page, north face of the Firehouse Arts Center from across the Merrimack River.
Left, south face of the original Lyceum and Market Hall, mid-nineteenth century.

The restored south facade and forecourt on Market Square.

The north-facing addition.

Section showing placement of theater auditorium.

Second floor, with theater.

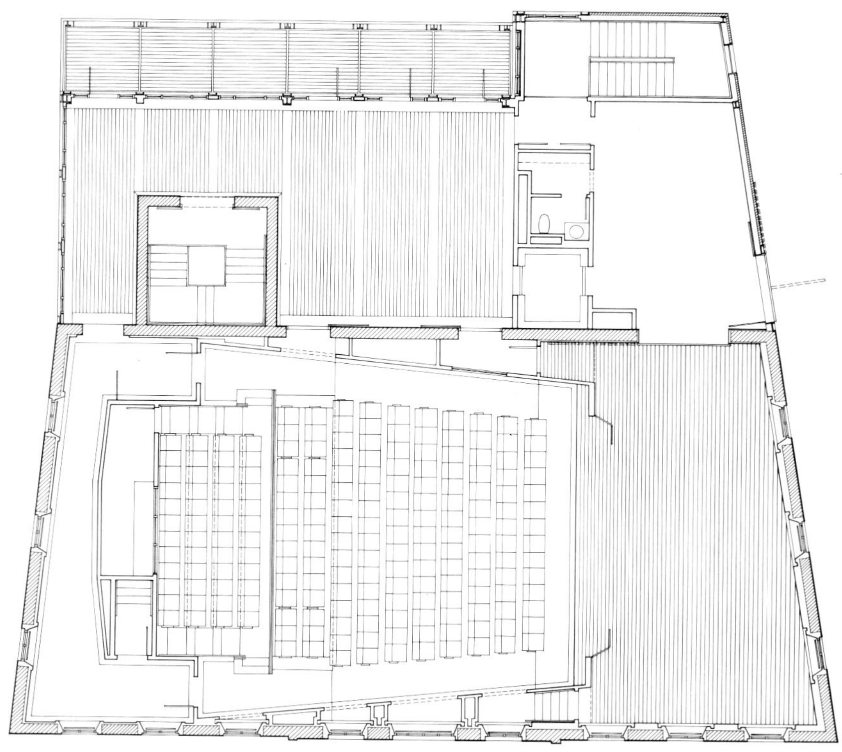

First floor, with gallery and café.

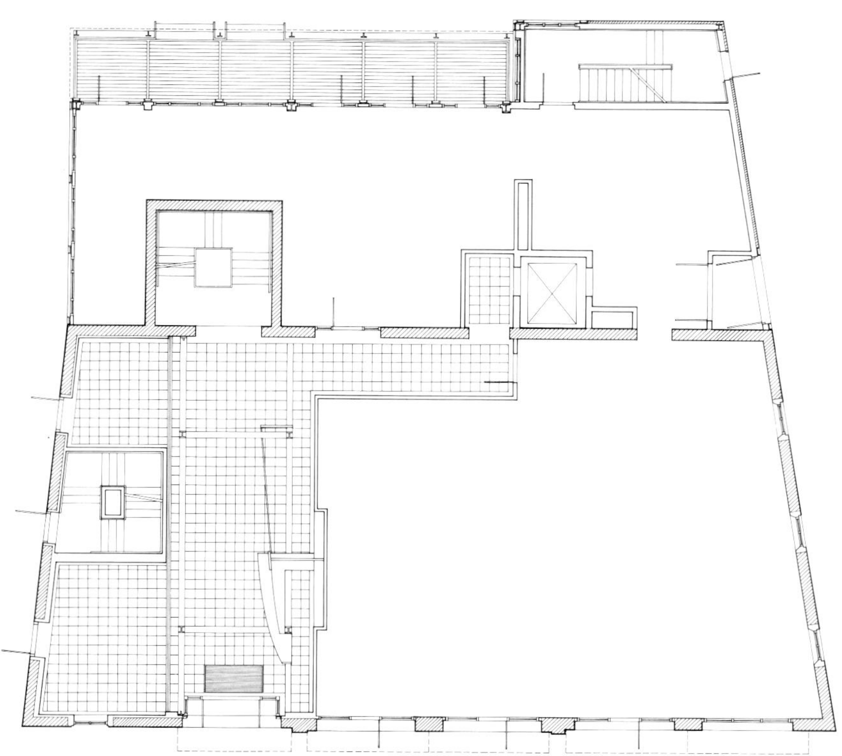

The east face of the Firehouse Before removing original low-level addition.

The original rear addition of the Firehouse.

View from north.

First and second-story porches facing the river; view from north-west.

Second-story porch
at theater upper
lobby, view to west.

First floor entry and exhibition gallery, detail. Below, second floor theater auditorium and stage.

Proctor Academy Fowler Learning Center

Andover, NH, 1992-1995

Proctor Academy is situated in a small rural town with many of its buildings in traditional New England white clapboard, in a typical informal arrangement. Schwartz/Silver's commission was to design a new learning center for the school, containing an 800 square meter library, a computer center, two classrooms and eleven tutorial rooms. At a private secondary school the challenge for the library component of this project was to provide services and easy supervision of an entirely young adult population with access to 60,000 volumes.

With a teaching philosophy strongly based in individual tutorials, the school intended that the new Fowler Learning Center & Library should have an additional role as a social focus for the students, inclusive of all learning styles and abilities. The facility is therefore sited between the main classroom and administrative buildings, and the gym and dining hall, where students pass by and through it several times a day. The social function of the facility is further supported by an open atrium, which connects the three floors, organizing circulation within the building, and serving as gallery and break-out space for a conference room. The exterior appearance of the building, while modern in style, is designed to create a strong connection to the rest of the campus; sympathetic both in its massing, and in its white clapboard exterior and window details. The interior space of the library is modeled after a New England meeting house, a high-ceilinged single volume. The structural frame visually separates the central stack space from a row of study carrels and reading areas along the perimeter. Daylight, through the south-facing windows, is controlled by large shutters, and is reflected by a white-painted ceiling deep into the library space. The interior finishes emphasize the rural character of the school, with an exposed heavy timber fir frame, fir floors and stairs, and cherry trim and casework.

Client:
Proctor Academy
Structural Engineer:
Charles Chaloff Consulting Engineers
Mechanical Engineer:
Yeaton Associates
Electrical Engineer:
C & M Engineering
Civil Engineer:
Lepene Engineering
Lighting Consultant:
Doug Baker
Contractor:
Engelberth Construction, Inc.
Landscape:
Bill Hoffman
Photographer:
Richard Mandelkorn
Schwartz/Silver Project Team:
Warren Schwartz
Robert Miklos
David Stern
Rania Matar
Jonathan Traficonte
Mark Schatz

Opposite page, view of east facade across the pond, which is the focal point of the campus; below, view of south facade.
Left, neighboring campus buildings, many of which informed the design.

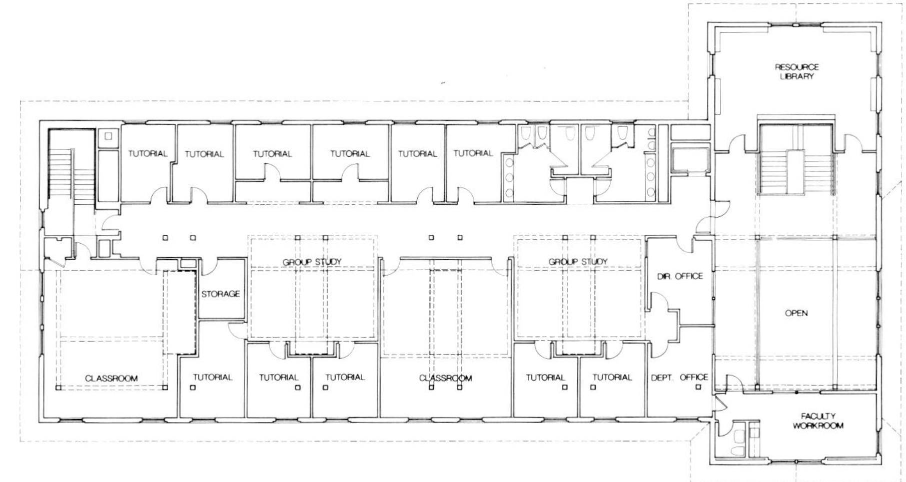

Second floor teaching facilities.

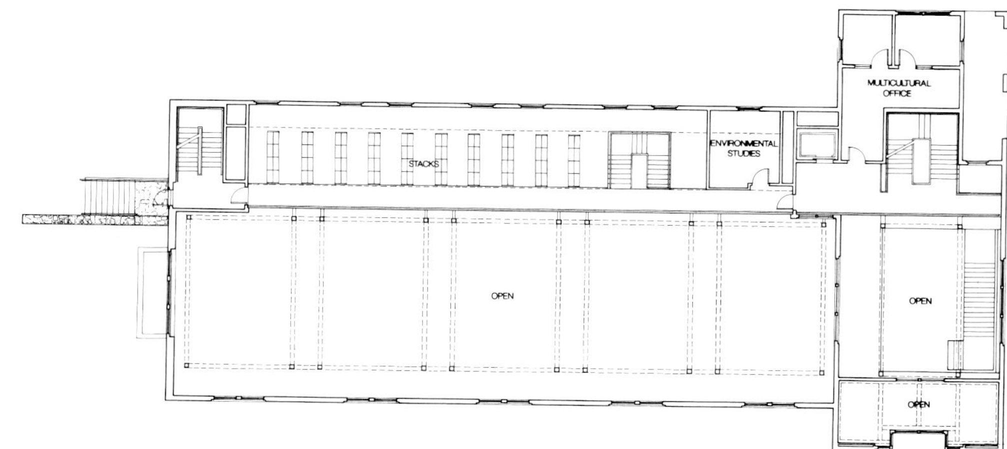

Mezzanine floor of library with passage out to dining hall.

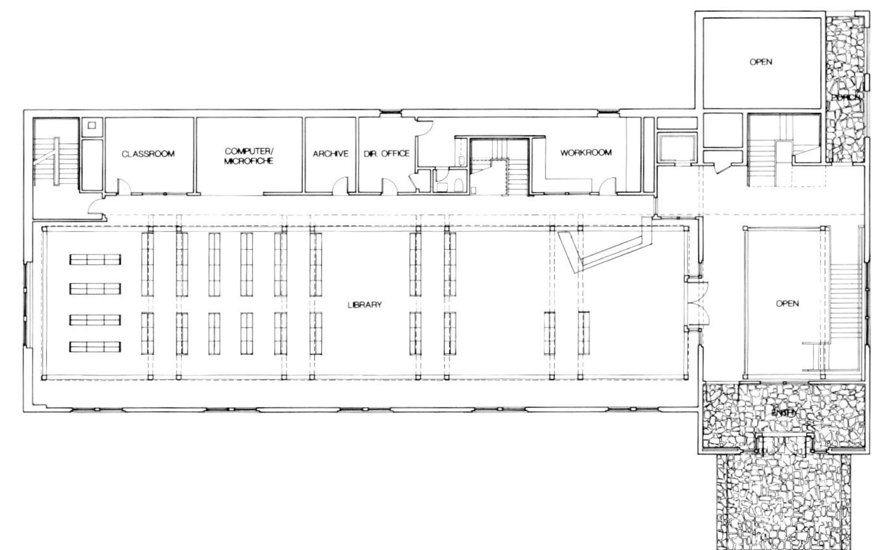

First floor library.

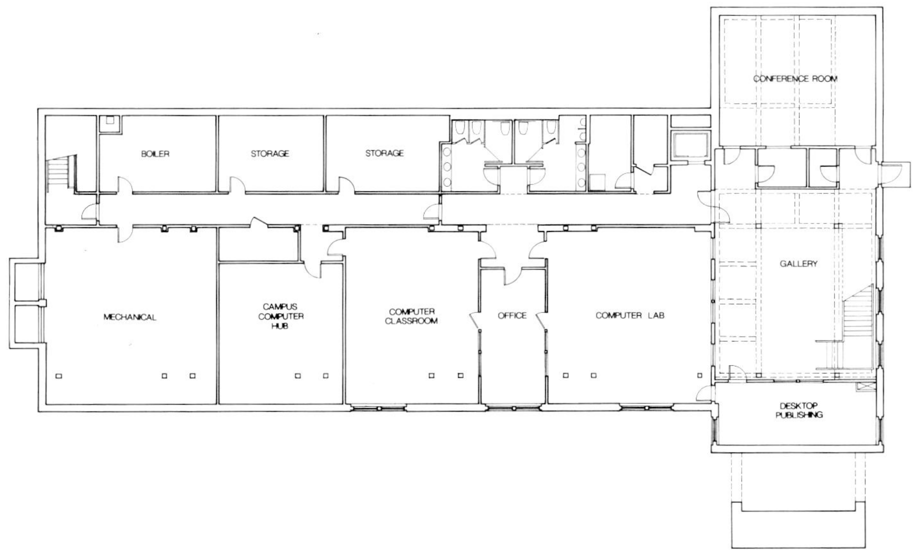

Ground floor computer center.

Detail of south facade of Fowler Learning Center and Library.

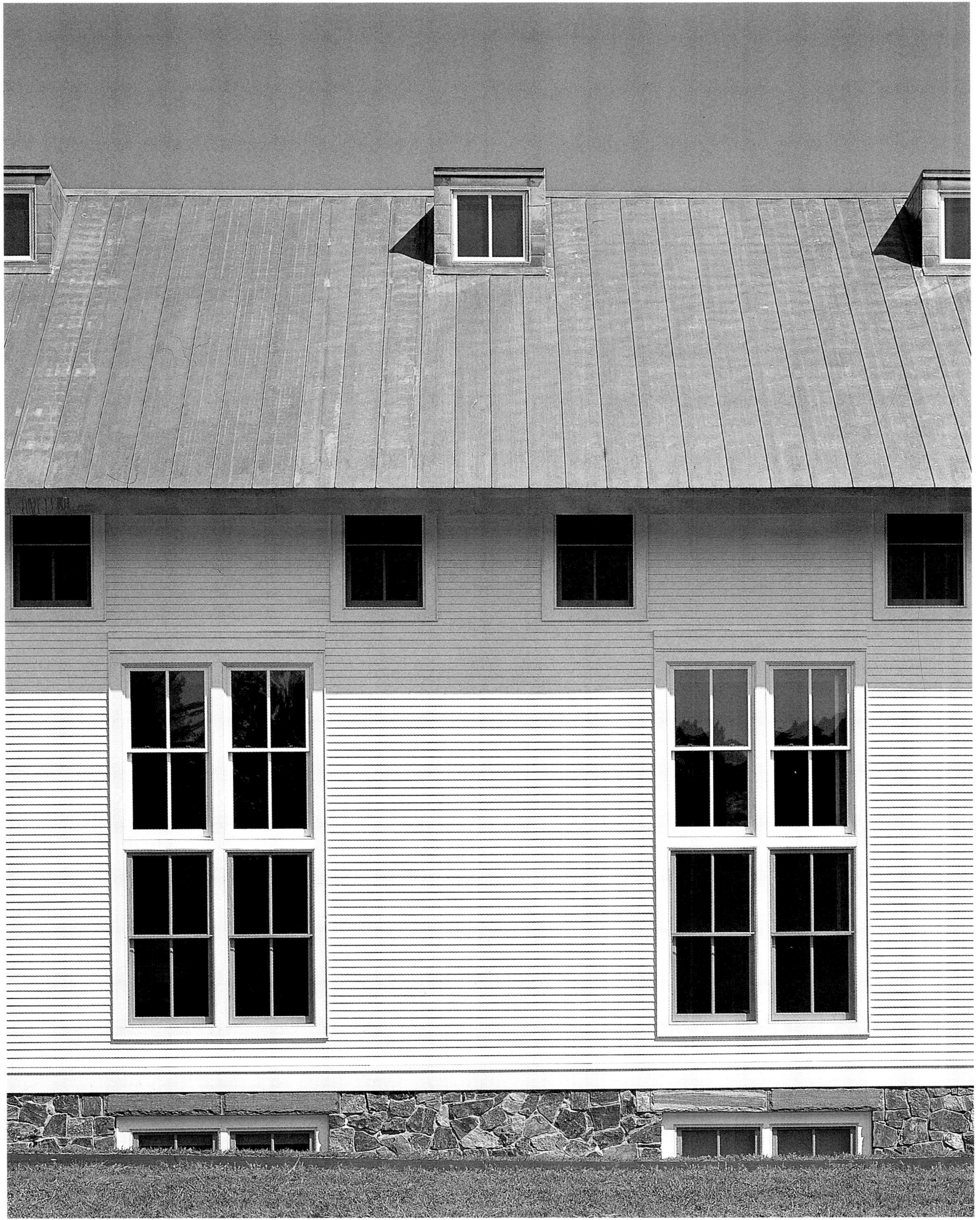

View of atrium from
mezzanine passage.

Below, stair to second floor. Bottom, view of atrium from ground floor gallery.

Below, second floor classroom. Bottom, reading area in the library.

CHELSEA
TRIAL
COURT

Chelsea Trial Court

Chelsea, MA, 1992-1999

In 1992 a Commission on the Future of the Courts was submitted to the Commonwealth of Massachusetts expressing its vision of a reinvented justice system. The new Chelsea Trial Court was commissioned in the spirit of realizing that vision: to bring the presence of state government into the heart of a city in a way that holds the neighborhood together, increases access to public services, and updates the traditions of monumental courthouse architecture.

The site consists of almost two entire blocks, located between a brick rowhouse neighborhood and a nineteenth-century commercial district, and backing up to an off-ramp from the Tobin Bridge, the main highway across the harbor to Boston. The front facade of the building negotiates the transition along the main street from commercial to residential, through its right-to-left composition of cylindrical entry, rectangular public lobby and courtrooms, and the smaller, nearly freestanding mass of the arraignment court. The round form of the entry, and the alternating pier-and-window pattern of the main lobby, evoke the traditional courthouse rotunda and colonnade, and accommodates the building to its urban setting.

Inside, a three-story public lobby, with an open stair along the exterior window wall, provides access to public services and courtrooms. Outside the courtrooms, high-backed seating areas allow semi-private spaces for attorneys to consult with their clients, or for families to gather. The monumental windows, piers and entry forms that give the exterior its impressive scale also shape the character of these public spaces, filling them with light, sheltering them from the activity on the street, and offering views across the neighborhood and harbor, to the skyline of Boston.

Opposite page, view of courthouse from the main commercial district.

Client:
Commonwealth of Massachusetts
Structural Engineer:
Charles Chaloff Consulting Engineers
MEP Engineer:
Shekar & Associates, Inc.
Civil Engineer:
Bryant Associates, Inc.
Environmental Consultant:
TGG Environmental, Inc.
Acoustic Consultant:
Cavanaugh Tocci Associates, Inc.
Lighting Consultant:
Peter Coxe Associates
Interiors Consultant:
Leslie Saul Associates
Signage Consultant:
John Roll Associates
Project Review:
SEA Consultants, Inc.
Contractor:
R. W. Granger & Sons, Inc.
Landscape Architect:
Berarducci Rutledge Landscape Architects
Photographers:
Peter Vanderwarker (p. 42)
Schwartz/Silver
Schwartz/Silver Project Team:
Warren Schwartz
Randolph Meiklejohn
Jon Traficonte
Steven Gerrard
Kathleen Lindstrom
Angela Ward Hyatt
Peter Kleiner
John Sheetz
Kazuyo Oda

Below, view from the southeast, with the arraignment court in the fareground. Bottom, lobby and entrance from the main stairway.

Below left, lobby stairway.
Below right and bottom, views of the arraignment court.

Level 3.

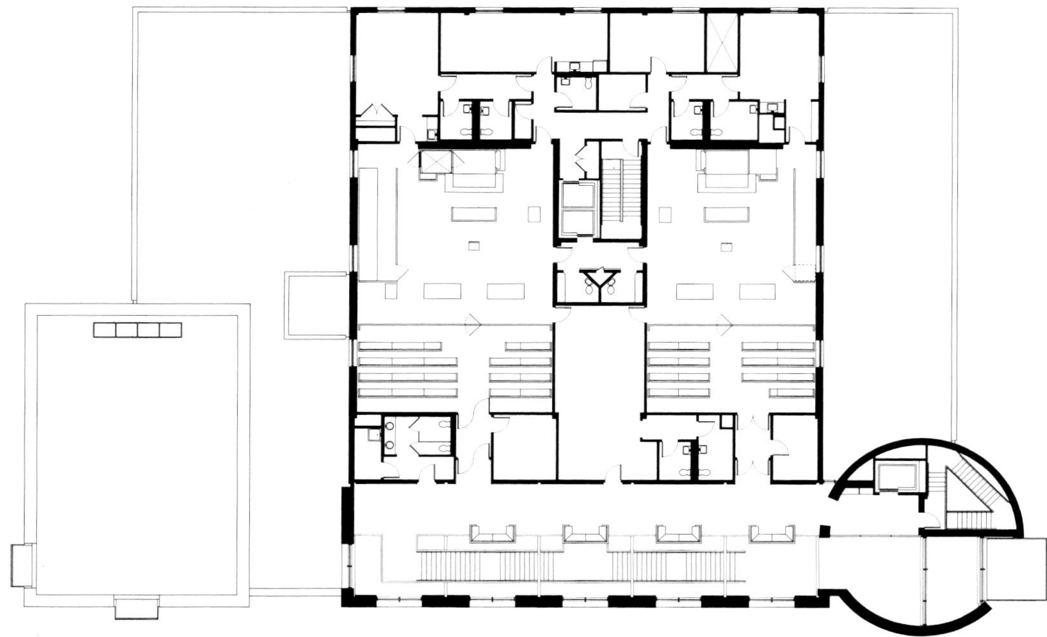

Level 2.

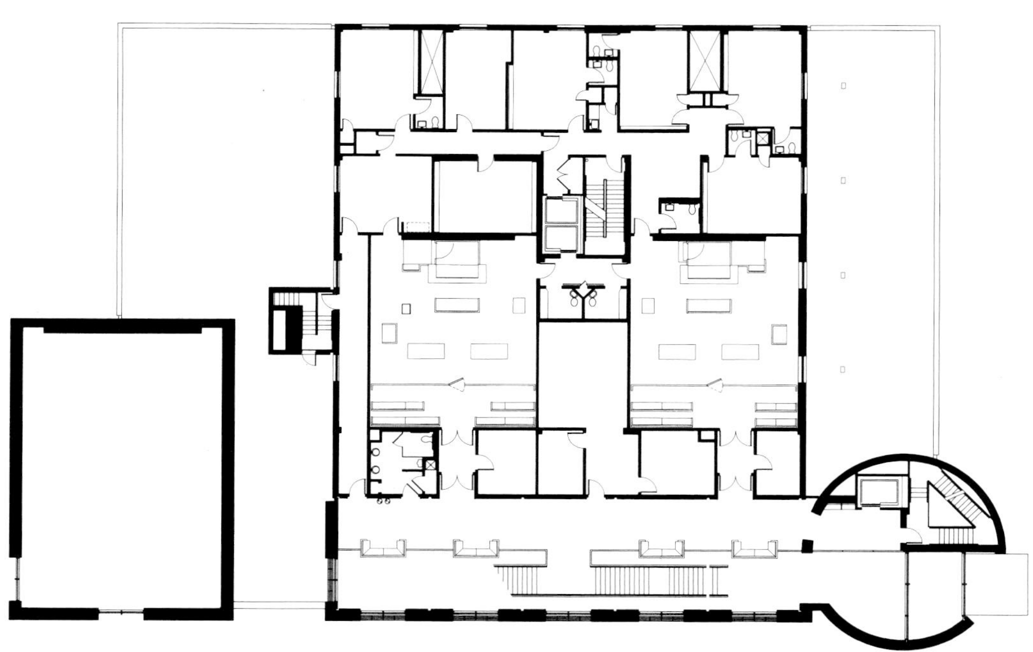

Level 1.

Courthouse entrance, with the Tobin Bridge in the background.

View from the northwest.

House on the Coast

USA, 1993-1998

At the cape of a small bay on a rocky coastline, the site of this large, two-story residence is graced with extraordinary views of the open ocean.

Responding to this exceptional vantage point is fundamental to the design conception of the house: its arcing form follows the line of water round into the bay, creating panoramic views of sea and sky. Counterposed to this predominant line is a second arc, facing the land and presenting the main entry to the house. The rooms inside are arranged along the two opposing curves, so that the whole form of the house is experienced as much from the interior as it is from the exterior. The spatial organization has the effect of producing a pointed internal atrium shaped like a canoe.

This creates a dynamic potential of echo and counterpoint in these curvilinear forms which is then developed further. Where one end of the house swoops up, it is met by the movement of the atrium clerestory, curving in the opposite direction. Openings, windows and terraces are created by curves peeling away from one another, interrupting, overlapping and crossing over, like the interplay of waves against shore. The principle is carried through to the smallest details of door handles and shelving. The resulting sense of motion is not only sympathetic to the water but also to the flight of the seabirds and the billowing sails of the yachts that occasionally pass by.

Such an exposed location, facing the broad expanse of the ocean, allows for dramatically shifting qualities of daylight to be a special feature of the house. Light floods into the building through the atrium clerestory, the floor-to-ceiling windows on all sides of the house, and the glass curtainwall facing the ocean, which reaches nine meters at its highest point. Large expanses of white wall envelop these various sources of daylight to introduce the interplay of reflected light. Minute-by-minute changes in the luminosity of the sky and the constantly shifting color and texture of the ocean are captured and magnified by the house.

Client:
(withheld at owner's request)
Structural Engineer:
Sarkis Zerounian & Associates
Mechanical Engineer:
Fitzemeyer & Tocci, Inc.
Electrical Engineer:
Johnson & Stover Inc.
Smart House Consultant:
Symdex Systems
Lighting Consultant:
Ripman Lighting Consultants
Interior Design:
William Hodgins
Contractor:
Thoughtforms Corporation
Photographers:
Richard Mandelkorn
Schwartz/Silver (p. 48-9, 52-3)
Schwartz/Silver Project Team:
Warren Schwartz
David Stern
Kathleen Lindstrom
John Nakazawa
Christopher Ingersoll
Jonathan Traficonte
Lisa Iwamoto

Opposite page, aerial view from south-east.
Left, view from south.

Upper level.

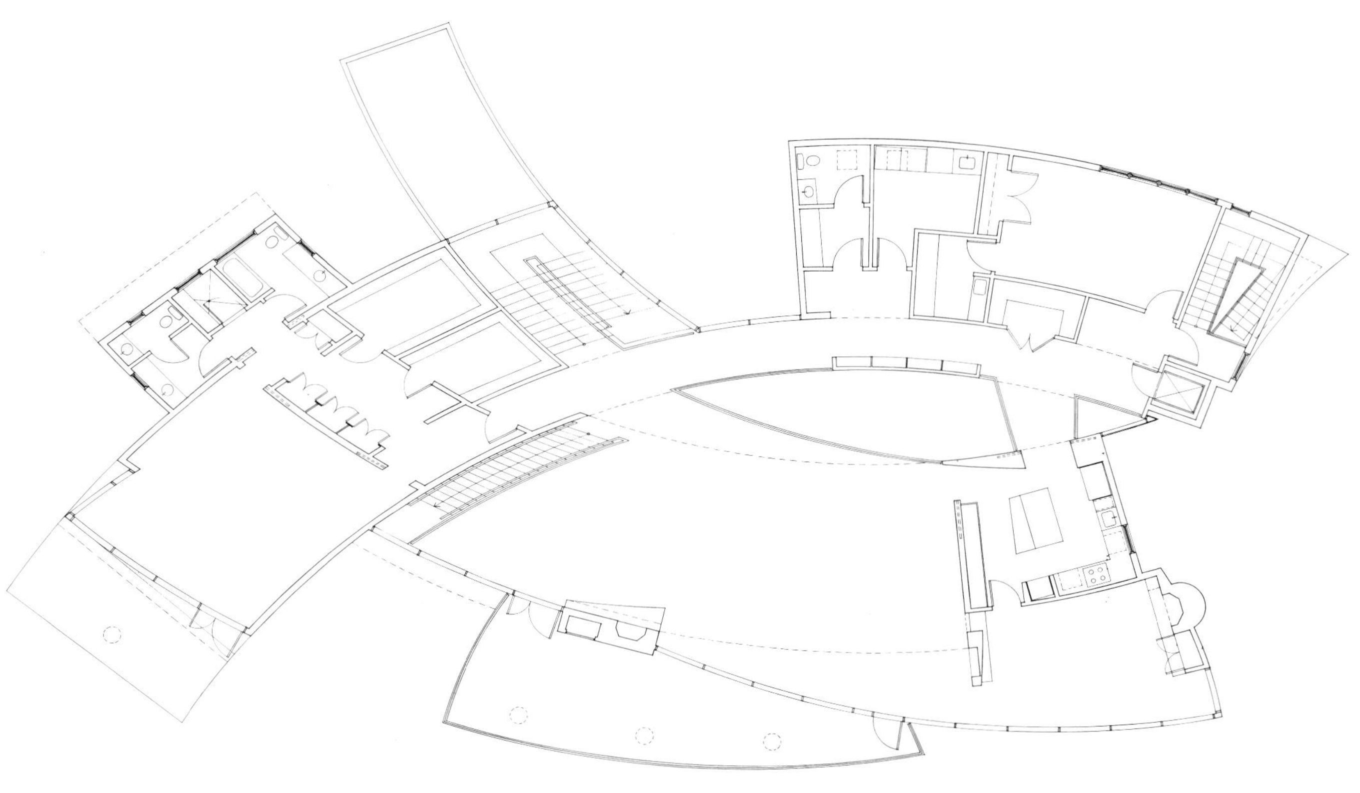

Lower level.

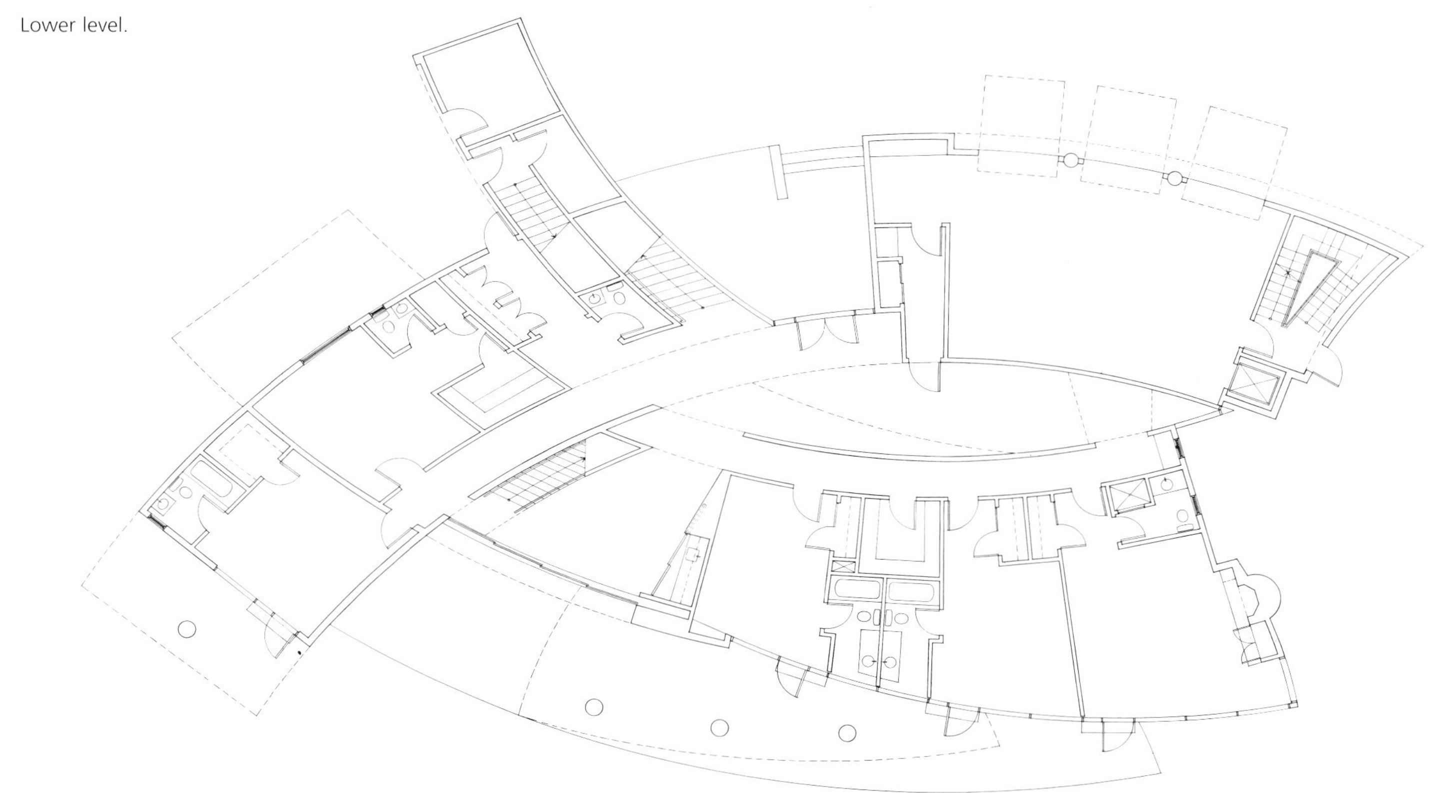

East elevation.

Below,
northeast corner.
Bottom,
west elevation.

Main entry.

Below, living/dining window-wall.
Bottom, view of atrium from entry.

Below, view from living/dining stairway.
Bottom, view West from living/dining.

View of atrium.

View from living/dining stairway.

COASTAL RHYTHMS
WHALE WATCH

New England Aquarium

Boston, MA, 1994-

The New England Aquarium, which set a world standard for aquarium design when it opened in 1969, started to redefine its mission in the early 1990s. Responding to the growing urgency for ecological awareness, a new emphasis was placed on educating the public, not just about the world of water, but about its relationship with the human world. Schwartz/Silver was engaged to develop a new architectural identity, which would expand and update the aquarium in support of the redefined mission.

Because the concept of the original building had been fundamentally inward looking, it had blank walls that closed off views to the outside. The master plan calls for two major additions, offering a connection back to the city on one side, and to the harbor on the other. The new design does not attempt to do away with the old concrete aquarium, but literally builds upon it, encrusting it the way new plant-life and crustaceans grab onto rocks. Angular forms, and surface materials which are by turns reflective and transparent, dramatically contrast with the neighboring condominium towers and brick buildings of Boston's waterfront district, as well as the rectilinear opacity of the original building. The first phase of Schwartz/Silver's master plan, the West Wing entrance and ticketing area, was completed by the firm in 1998. While not a direct representation of the ocean world, the elements of the building engage the imagination of visitors at the level of their own personal experience. The swiveling ventilation outlets in the lobby do not literally mimic barnacle forms, but they are unusual enough to demand interpretation. The exterior skin of the building is not recognizable as the surface of fish scales, but is suggestive of it. And the building forms in the entry plaza might be variously interpreted as the rock formations of undersea caves, the claws of a giant lobster, floating icebergs, or the hulls of ships. The connections that the building establishes between the human world and the world of water are therefore not merely physical but also emotional and psychological.

Opposite page, West Wing Entrance,
view from north-west.

Client:
The New England Aquarium
Exhibit Designer:
Lyons/Zaremba Inc.
Structural Engineer:
Weidlinger Associates, Inc.
MEP Engineer:
Syska & Hennessy
Civil Engineer:
Judith Nitsch Engineering, Inc.
Marine Engineer:
Childs Engineering Corp.
Lighting Designer:
H.M. Brandston & Partners, Inc.
Acoustic Consultant:
Jaffe Holden Scarbrough Acoustics, Inc.
Waterfront Consultant:
TAMS Consultants Inc.
Contractor:
Beacon Skanska Construction Company
Photographer:
Matt Wargo
Steve Turner (aerial)
Schwartz/Silver Project Team:
Warren Schwartz
Robert Silver
Christopher Ingersoll
Kathleen Lindstrom
Angela Ward Hyatt
Steven Gerrard
Nelson Liu
Mark McVay
Lisa Iwamoto
Sandra Saccone
Peter Kleiner
Randolph Meiklejohn
Robert Miklos
John Nakazawa
Scott Peltier
John Sheetz
Patricia Anahory Silva

COASTA

Left, gift shop and café addition from south.
Below from top, aerial view from north,
West Wing from south,
addition from west.

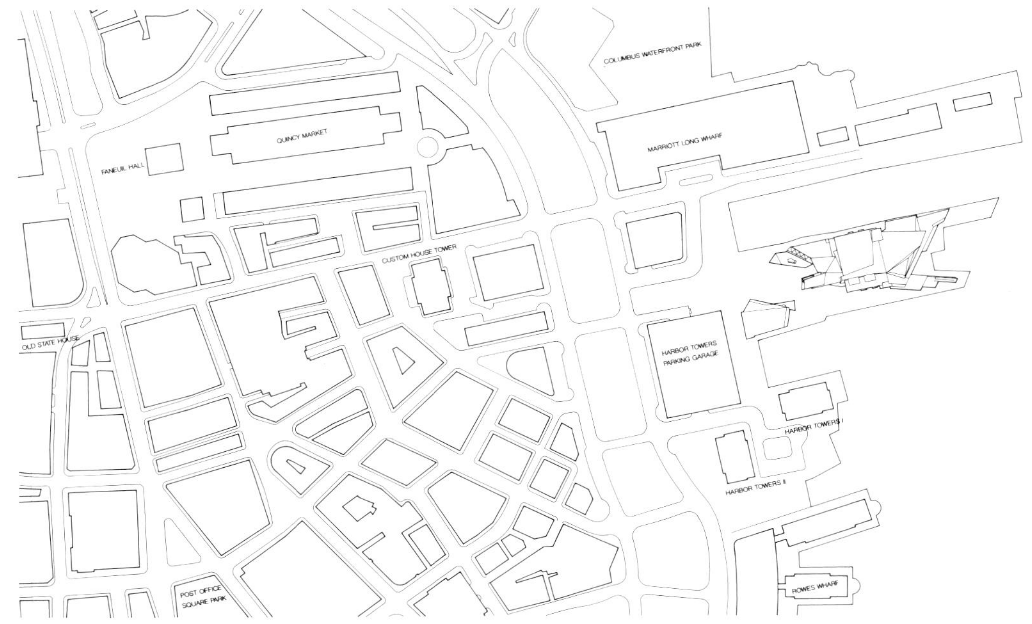

Site plan.

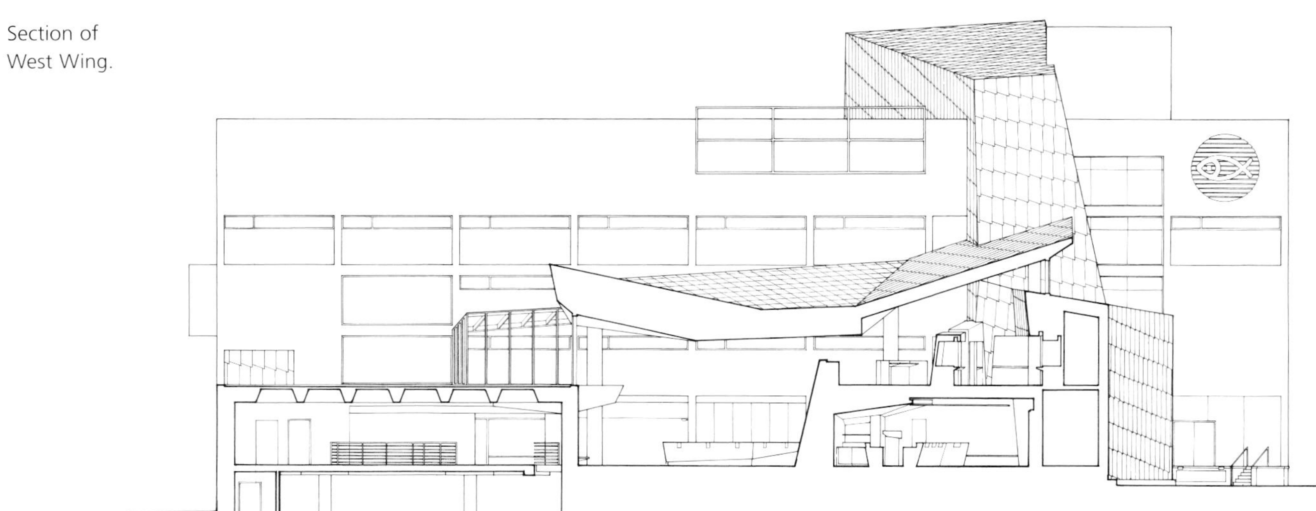
Section of West Wing.

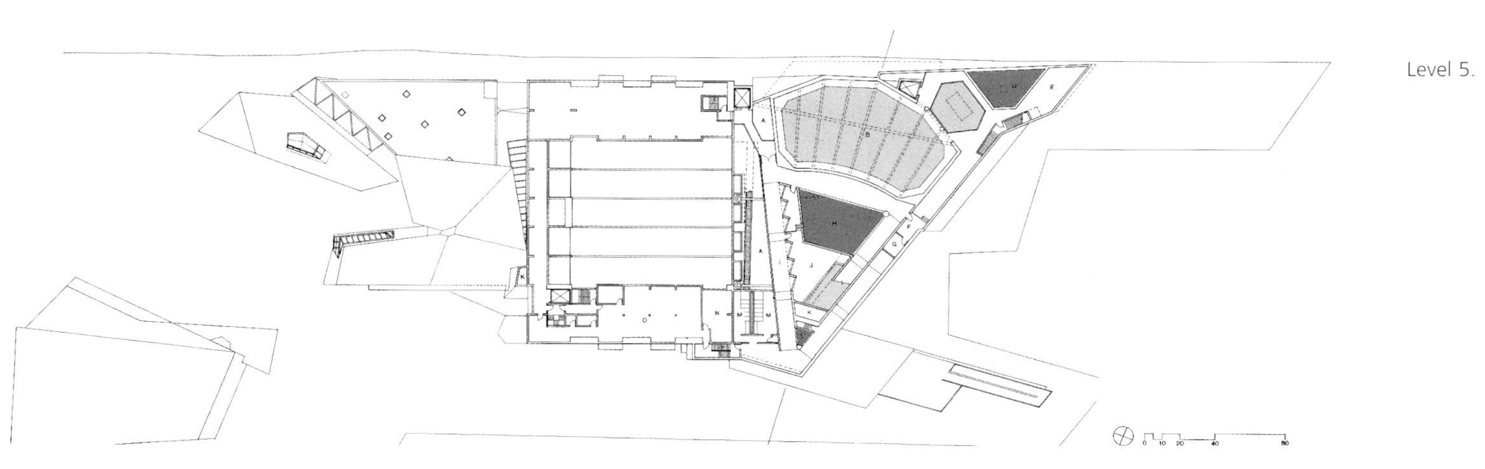

Level 5.

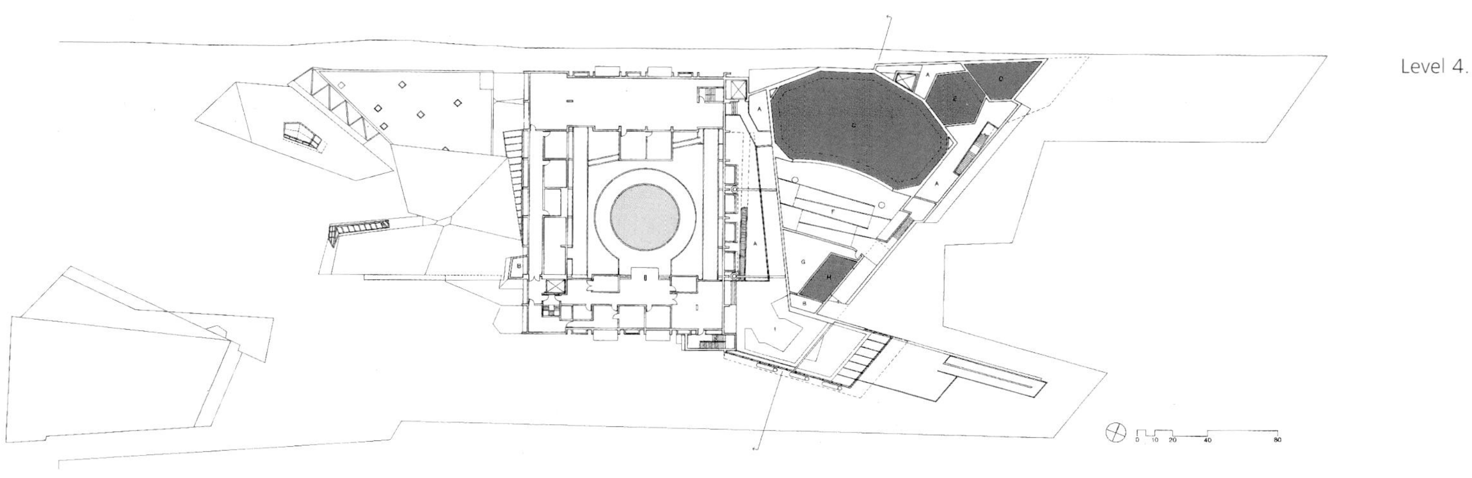

Level 4.

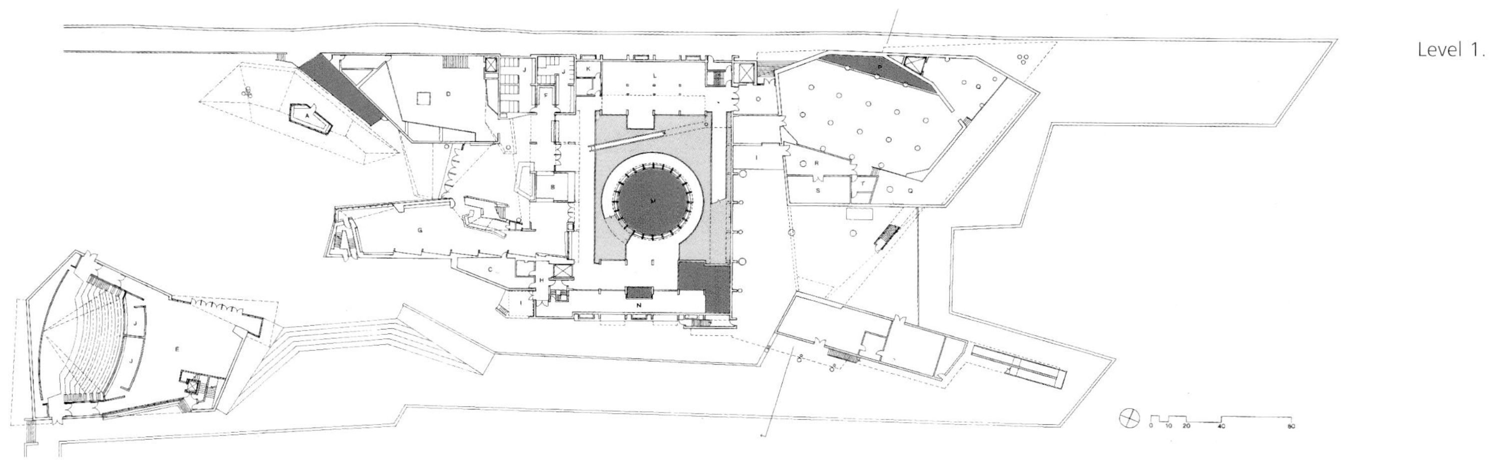

Level 1.

Opposite page, top, composite rendering of completed master plan; bottom, ticket booth canopy and seal tank. Left, West Wing from the entry plaza. Below, view across entry plaza to downtown Boston.

Entrance lobby with stairs up to café.

View of café and severy.

View from lobby back to ticket booth.

View over entry plaza from upper level café.

The Aquarium gift shop.

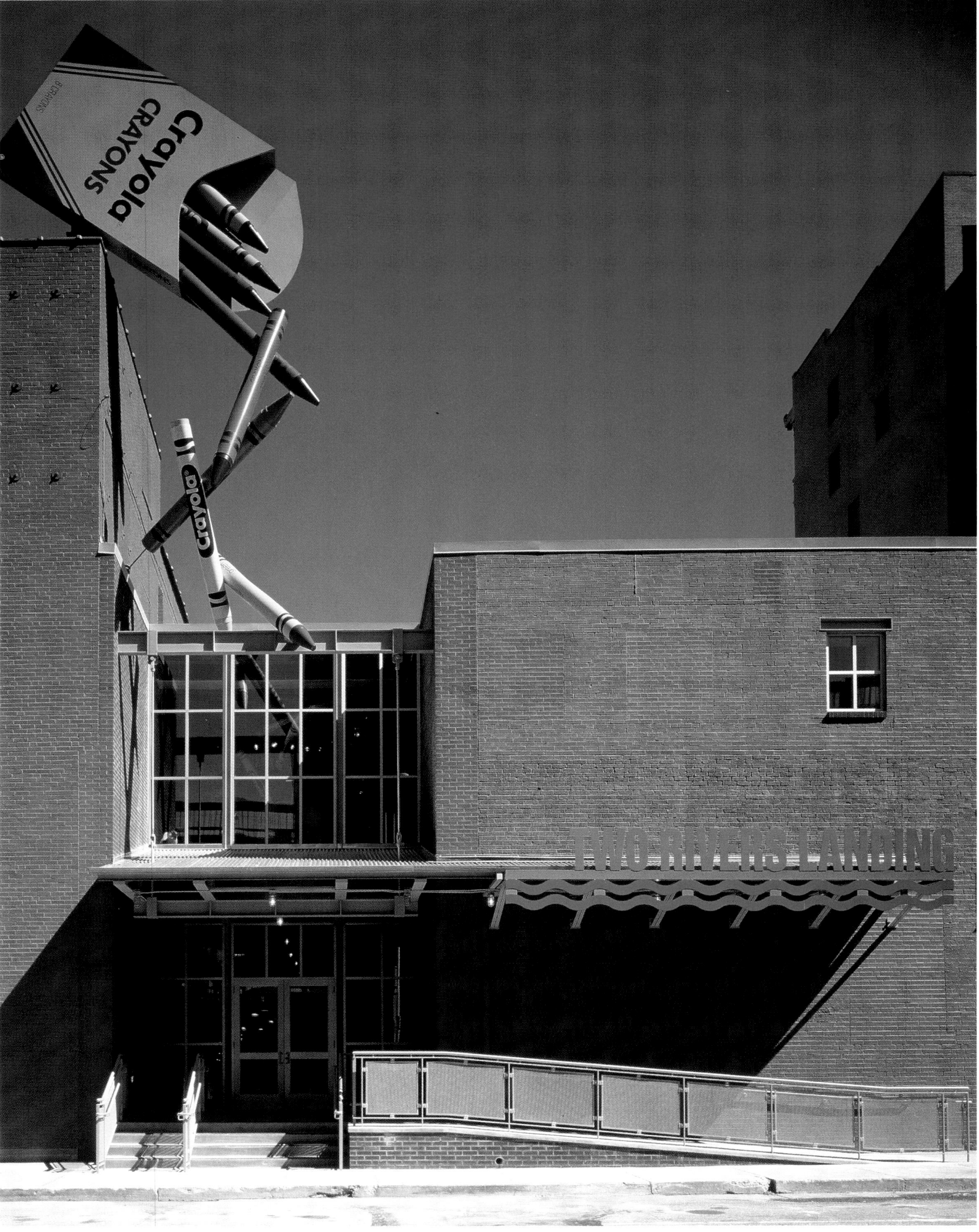
Crayola
CRAYONS
Crayola
TWO RIVERS LANDING

Two Rivers Landing

The National Canal Museum, The Crayola FACTORY, Easton, PA, 1994-1996

Easton is a small city in Eastern Pennsylvania that had once been a thriving industrial center. During the 1970s and 80s, like many American cities, its downtown went into decline, with storefronts boarded-up and widespread building vacancy. Two Rivers Landing is public/private initiative, the joint effort of several local organizations and corporations, to regenerate the city as a cultural attraction with the combined appeal of two museums: the Crayola FACTORY (highlighting the enormously popular crayons, manufactured locally) and the National Canal Museum (a museum already based in Easton). On the main square, a group of five abandoned buildings was acquired for the project, including a former department store. Together they offered the possibility of connecting the central shopping street to the city's main parking garage, although, with the limited budget for the project, they also brought the complications of varying floor heights and states of repair.

Schwartz/Silver's design strategy, responding to the need for low-cost, stripped-down interior spaces, makes the particular heritage of the urban context a feature of the project. The different floor heights of the buildings are emphasized by a sloping pedestrian bridge, whose design recalls old factory complexes in the area, and provides a landmark entry icon for the facility at the corner of the main square. For the two museums, which both focus on aspects of local heritage, this industrial aesthetic is appropriate and supportive. But more than this, the complex is designed, with interior details and strategically orchestrated views outside, to orient visitors to see what is valuable and appealing in the surroundings, instead of what is redundant and irrelevant. As a result, Two Rivers Landing is not only achieving record-breaking visitation but its success has spread throughout the downtown, spawning hundreds of new businesses close by.

Client:
Easton Economic Development Corporation
Design Architect:
Schwartz/Silver Architects, Inc.
Associated Architect:
Wallace & Watson Associates
Exhibit Designer:
Krent Paffett Associates
Structural Engineer:
Pany & Lentz Engineering Company
MEP Engineer:
Wallace & Watson Associates
Contractor:
Alvin H. Butz Inc.
Photographer:
Matt Wargo
Schwartz/Silver Project Team:
Robert Miklos
David Stern
Nelson Liu
Steve Gerrard
Jonathan Traficonte

Opposite page, rear Entrance, facing city parking garage.
Left, the two department store buildings before renovation.

Level 3.

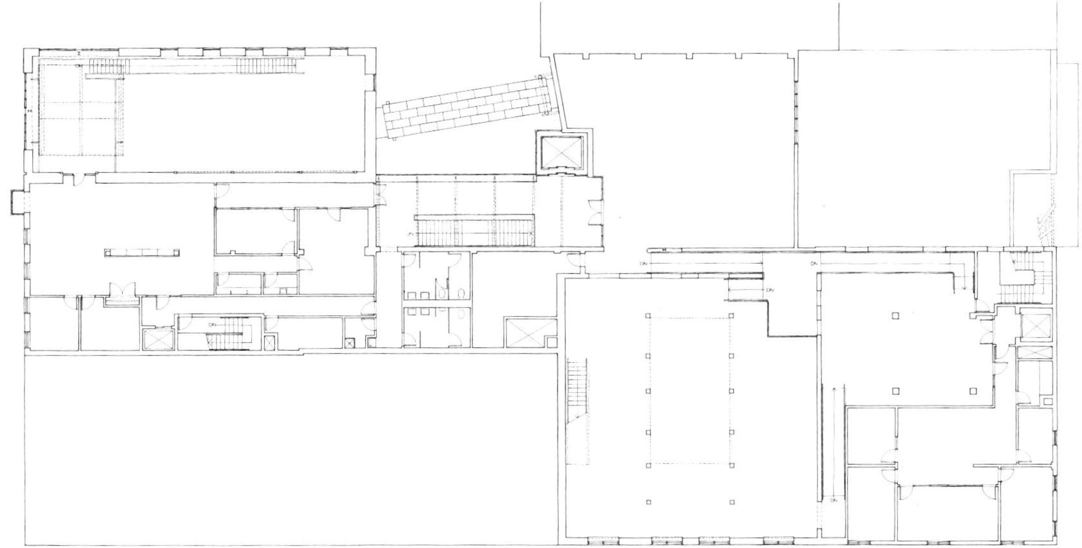

Level 2.

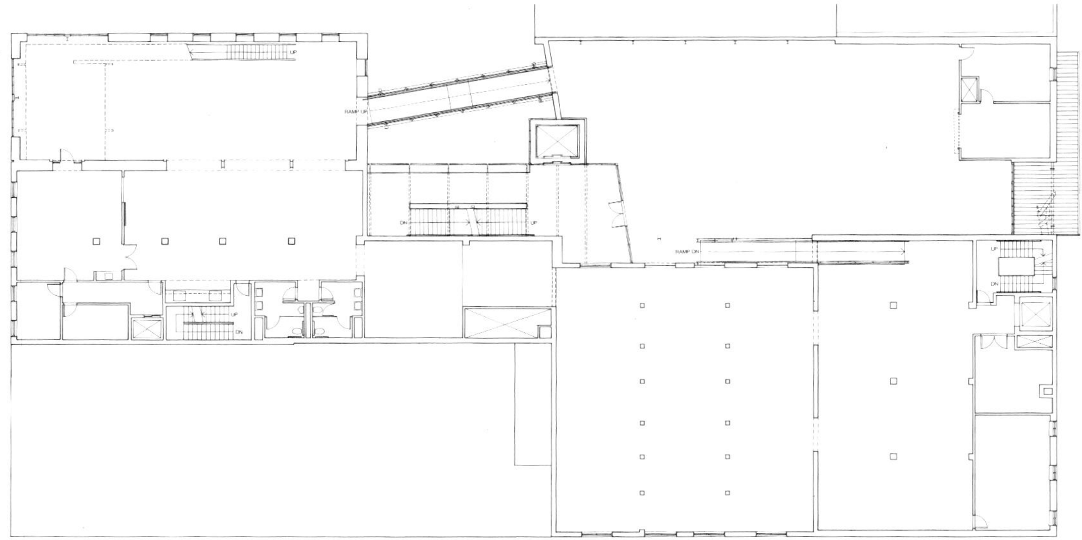

Level 1.

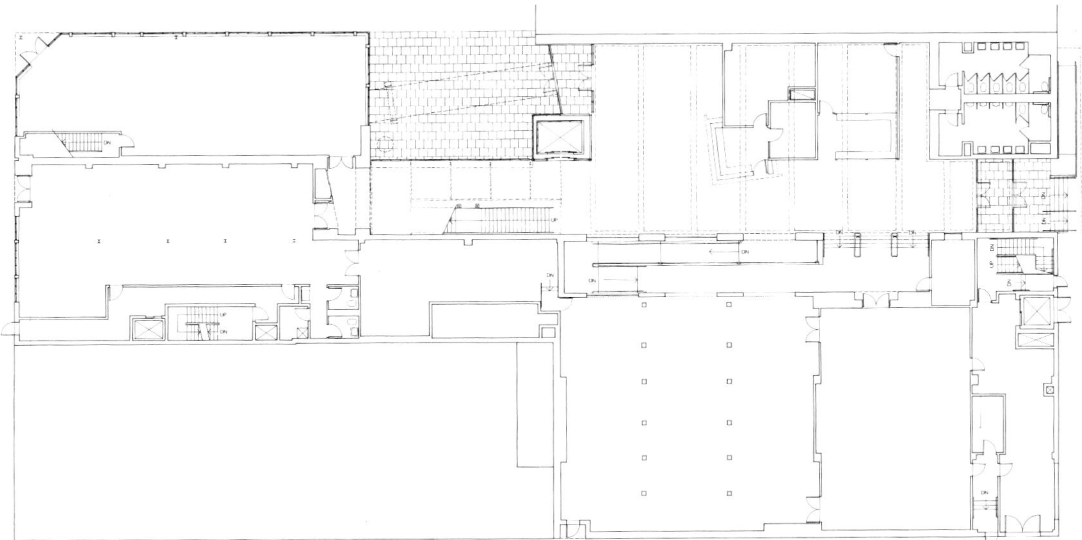

Below, south-north section.
Bottom, Northampton Street facade, replacing the former department store.

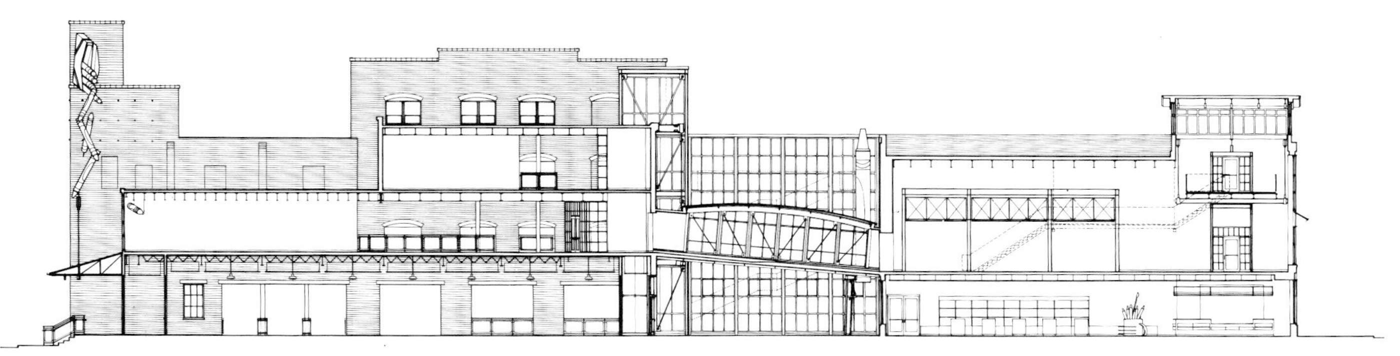

Pedestrian bridge and elevator tower, facing Centre Square.

Below, entry to Crayola FACTORY. Bottom, view of pedestrian bridge from second level passageway.

Below, stairway to pedestrian bridge. Bottom, 3-D Studio, first floor program area.

Sibley Hall Fine Arts Library

Cornell University
Ithaca, NY, 1995

Sibley Hall is one of Cornell's first academic buildings, and is one of the icons of this Ivy League institution. Built in the nineteenth century in the Beaux-Arts style, it forms the edge of Cornell's first campus quadrangle, the Arts Quad. It is one of four buildings housing the College of Architecture, Art & Planning. As part of a Master Plan for the College, Schwartz/Silver designed an addition to the rear of Sibley Hall to expand the existing Fine Arts Library and create a new lecture hall.

The original, completely frontal conception of the building resulted in a blank rear facade, creating an opportunity to introduce a new element that would not destroy the integrity of the original building. Where the views back over a deep gorge and one of the Finger Lakes now serve only as setting for Sibley Hall, the new addition makes these views a feature to be enjoyed by library users inside, and emphasizes a visual connection to the wider campus. As contrasting as it appears, the design of the addition is deferential to the historic building, reinforcing, rather than replacing its keynote features. The stack addition is transparent and glassy, creating a welcoming beacon for the College after dark. A stone screen, set back eight feet from the glass, protects the books. In this narrow intermediate zone, readers' areas have both access to the collections and the views. Below the stacks, at grade, are a new gallery space, adjoining central administration areas and the Dean's office. Under the gallery, is the new lecture hall, which would otherwise have represented too large a volume to incorporate in the main building. A sky lit gasket joins the addition to Sibley Hall, articulating a clear distinction between two contrasting styles. The tilted roof canopy slopes back to the dome, reinforcing the status of the original building as the focus of the College.

Client:
Cornell University
Structural Engineer:
LeMessurier Consultants
MEP Engineer:
BR+A Consulting Engineers
Schwartz/Silver Project Team:
Warren Schwartz
Robert Silver
Mark Schatz
Lisa Iwamoto
Scott Peltier

Opposite page, working model: north elevation (rear facade of Sibley Hall). Left, front facade of Sibley Hall.

Level 4.

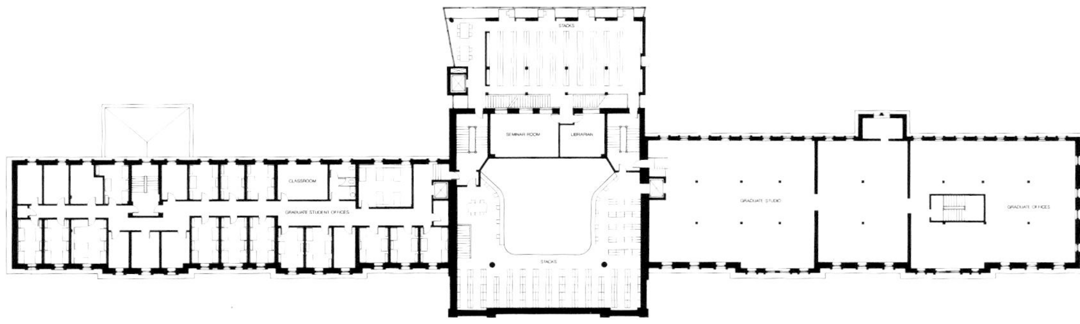

Level 3.

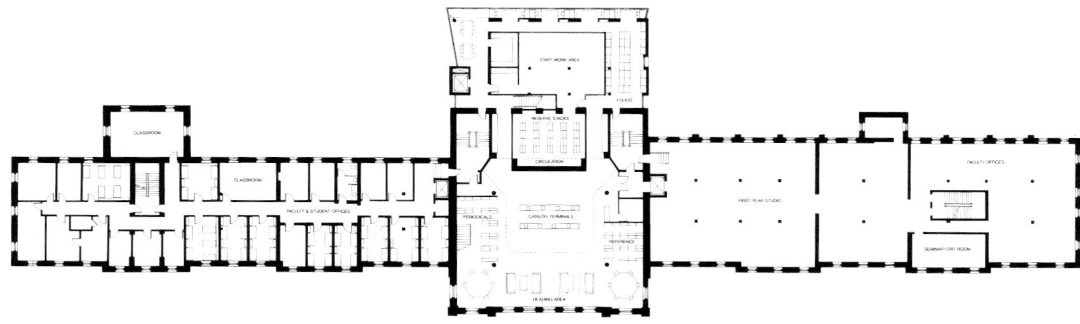

Level 2.

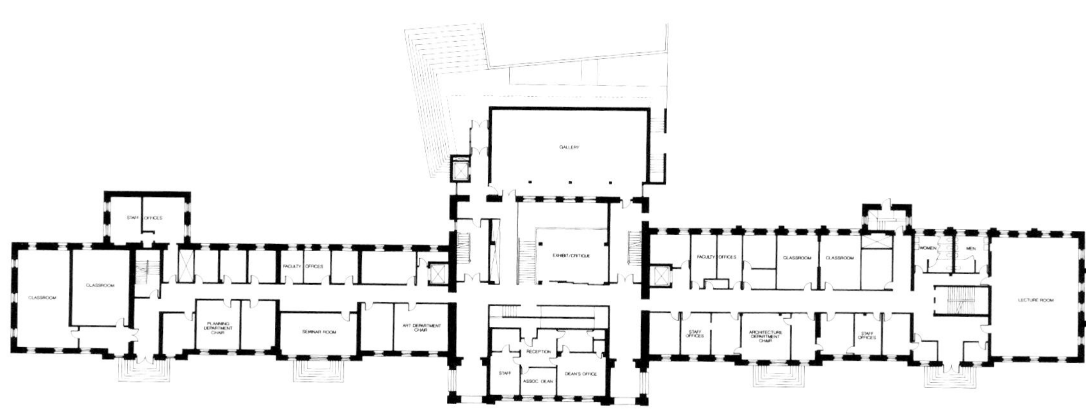

Level 1.

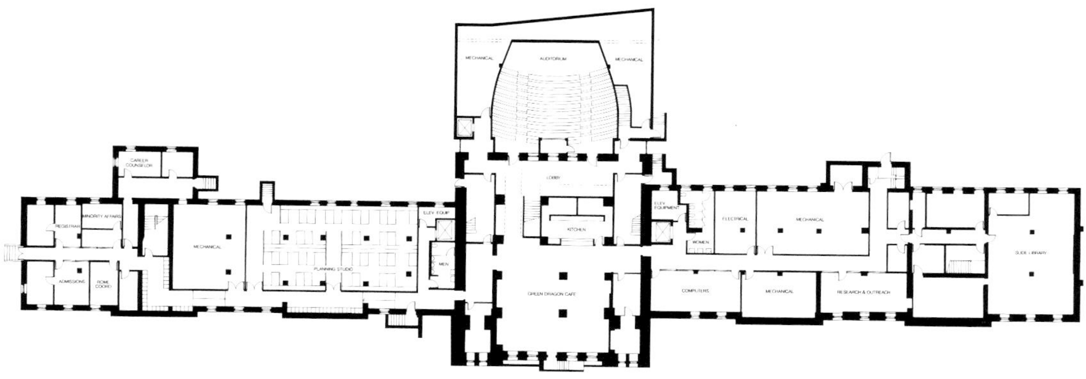

Below, north-south section.
Bottom, addition in campus context.

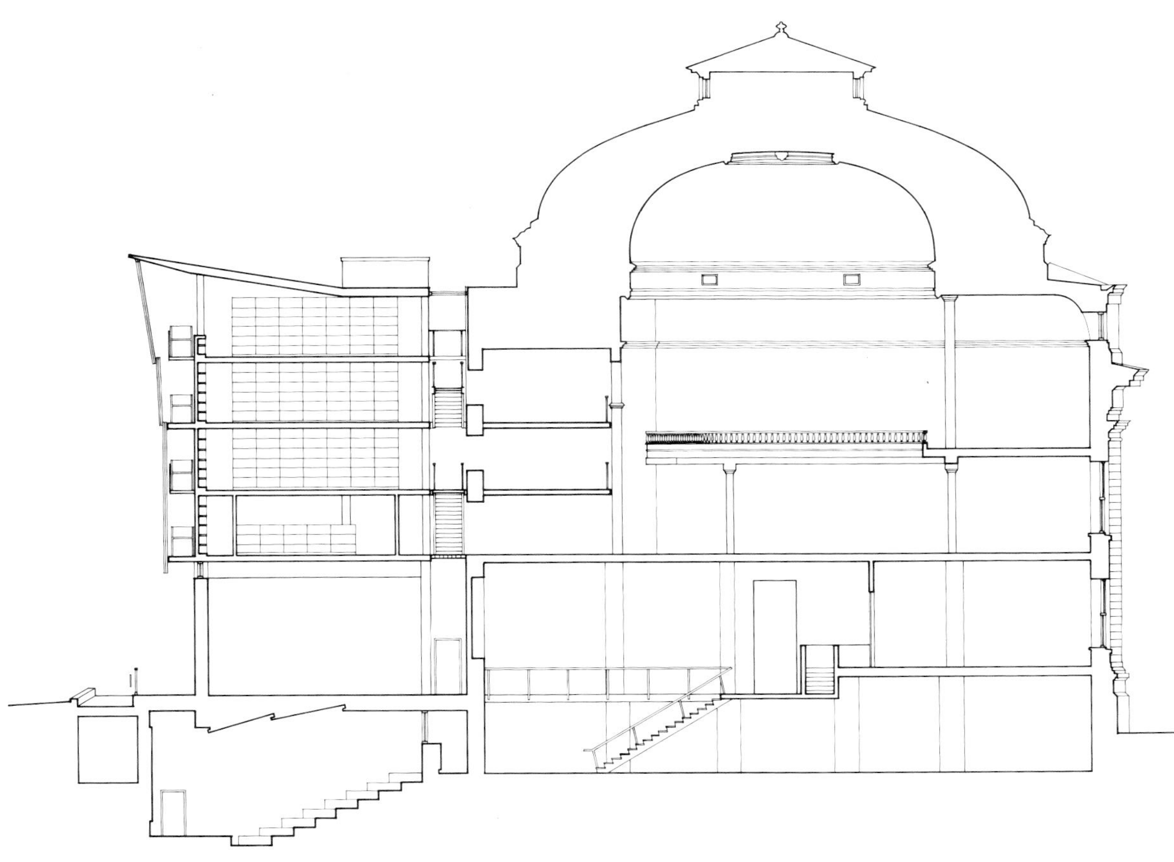

West elevation,
section through
Sibley Hall.

Detail of new
north facade.

Hyde Park Branch Library
Boston Public Library

Boston, MA, 1996-2000

Like the town libraries established by Carnegie philanthropy in the late nineteenth century, the original Hyde Park Library followed a Classical Revival model to establish its authority as a municipal landmark. With a grand portico entrance at the top of a broad flight of stone stairs, it was designed to communicate the privilege of education and knowledge to the local population. Apart from a small, one-story addition to the north side of the library, built in 1900, the building remained essentially unchanged until the expansion designed by Schwartz/Silver.

The glass addition to the south side of the building is a carefully orchestrated counterpoint to the historic library. Although the program area produced by the expansion is more than double that of the original building, the addition is visually equal in proportion to it, quietly deferring to the prominence of the portico. This was achieved by creating two small brick additions as bookends to the original building – on the north, modifying the addition of 1900; and on the south, mirroring it. Extra program area was also created by excavating a new basement floor under the building, which, because of the sloping topography of the site, could lead into above-ground space in the lower level of the new construction. The children's library is at this level, opening onto a reading garden, designed in an informal, almost rural character as an oasis of calm in a bustling urban neighborhood. The transparency of the upper two floors of the addition, where books and activity can easily be seen from the street, compensates for the fundamental aloofness of the original library, making it open and welcoming to potential readers. And yet the historic character of the original building, and the special qualities of its restored interior spaces, are respectfully highlighted by the addition. The library communicates its significance to the community by embodying both its past and its present.

Client:
City of Boston, Boston Public Library
Structural Engineer:
Charles Chaloff Consulting Engineers
Geotechnical Engineer:
Geotechnical Consultants, Inc.
MEP Engineer:
TMP Consulting Engineers
Historic Preservation:
Preservation Technology, Inc.
Contractor:
Boston Building & Bridge
Landscape:
Richard Burck Associates
Photographer:
Steve Rosenthal (p. 84, p. 87)
Schwartz/Silver Project Team:
Robert Miklos
David Stern
Angela Ward Hyatt
Peter Kleiner
Randolph Meiklejohn

Opposite page, south facade with children's garden.
Left, library building before expansion.

Views of
west facade.

Detail of
east facade
south-east corner.

Level 2.

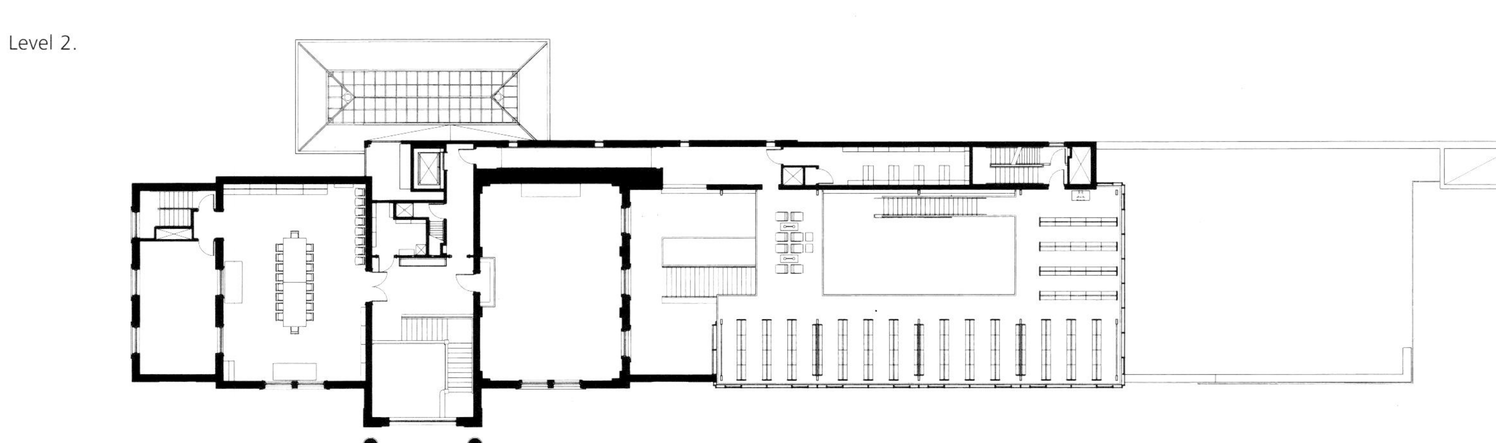

Level 1.

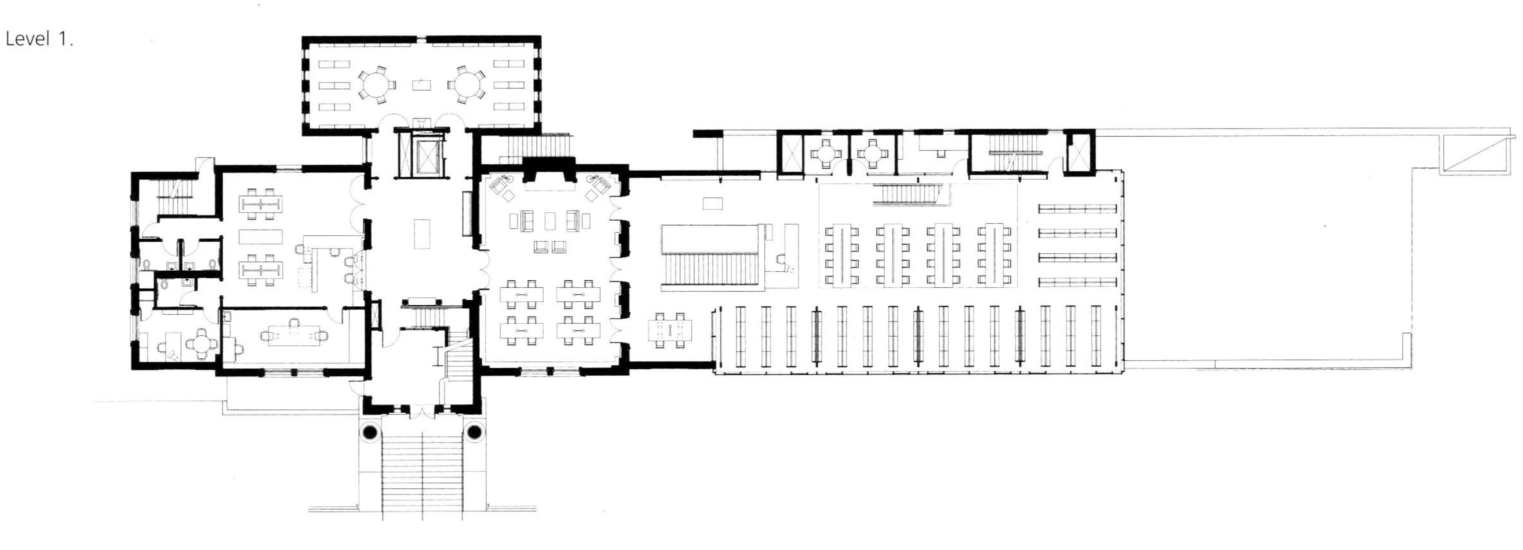

Level 0.

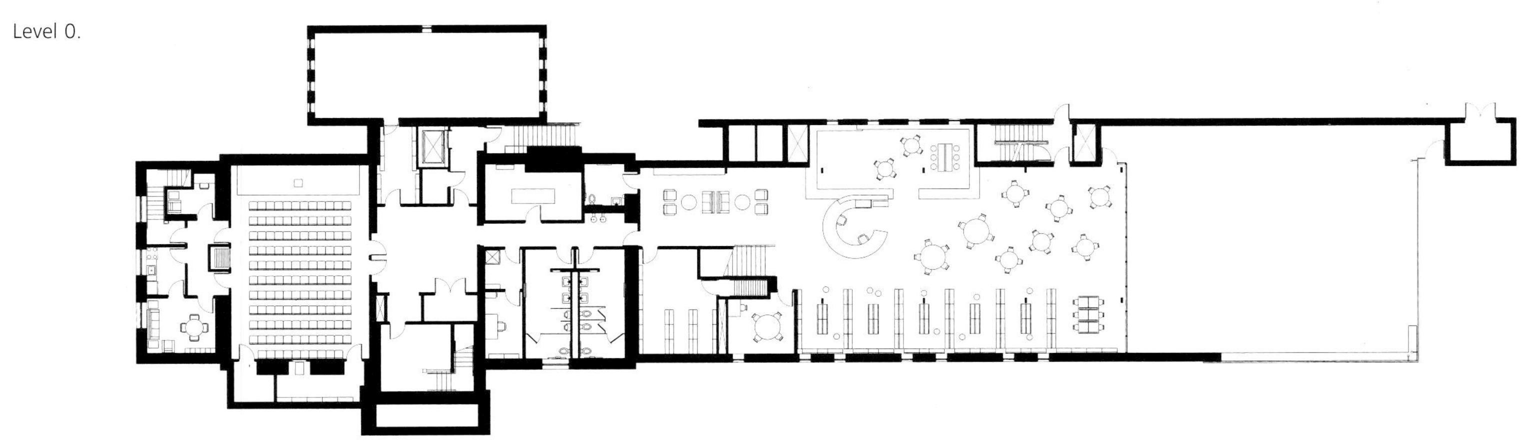

Below, south facade, with Reading Garden. Bottom, Children's Room, with view through to garden.

Views of Adult reading room.

PN-PR
PN
ML-ND
ND-PN
KF-ML

Farnsworth Art Museum

The Wyeth Center

Rockland, ME, 1997-1998

Located in the center of a harbor town, the Farnsworth Art Museum's collections have focused on New England, and specifically the Maine Coast, as a formative influence on American painting. Historic buildings are also part of the collections, including the famous Olson House (the subject of several paintings by Andrew Wyeth), the Cooper House, and the Farnsworth Family Homestead. Schwartz/Silver's work for the Museum was precipitated by the desire to create a special center for the highly popular, Maine-inspired works of several generations of the Wyeth family: Andrew Wyeth, his father, the illustrator N.C. Wyeth, and his painter son, James Wyeth.

A former church, across the street from the rest of the museum buildings, appealed to the Wyeths as an evocative and appropriate place to exhibit their work. Schwartz/Silver's project was not only to adapt and renovate the church in ways that would resonate with their paintings, but also to establish a meaningful connection with the museum facility across the street, by recreating it as a coherent campus. This way, the variety of building types and styles could become a strong identifying feature of the museum, rather than a confusing weakness.

To enclose the campus, and form a natural visitor path towards the church, Schwartz/Silver designed a long, narrow, barn-like building housing the new Wyeth Study Center. This creates a correspondingly long courtyard, leading down the campus towards the church. The courtyard is immediately visible on entering through the new entrance lobby; a transparent glass and steel block in a contrasting modern style, which demarcates an aperture along the street edge through which to enter the museum complex. At the far end of the Study Center is a small storage building, whose vernacular stone construction contributes yet another contrast in building styles. The ensemble effect emphasizes the Maine context, in all its heterogeneous history, as the frame through which the artwork can be experienced and understood.

Client:
The Farnsworth Art Museum
Structural Engineer:
Ocmulgee Associates, Inc.
MEP Engineer:
Allied Engineering, Inc.
Civil Engineering:
Coffin Engineering and Surveying
Contractor:
H.E. Callahan Construction Co.
Oliver Builders, Inc.
Landscape:
CBA Landscape Architects
Photographers:
Brian Vanden Brink (p. 94 top, p.95 bottom, p.96)
Schwartz/Silver Project Team:
Robert Miklos
Warren Schwartz
Robert Silver
Randolph Meiklejohn
Nelson Liu
Anne Filson
Matthew Littell
Steven Gerrard

Opposite page, the Wyeth Center is housed in several buildings, including a former church at the west end of the campus.

Below, site plan of new museum campus, showing relationship to church galleries.
Bottom left, rendering of new museum campus, viewed from church galleries.
Bottom right, the former church housing the Wyeth Center galleries.

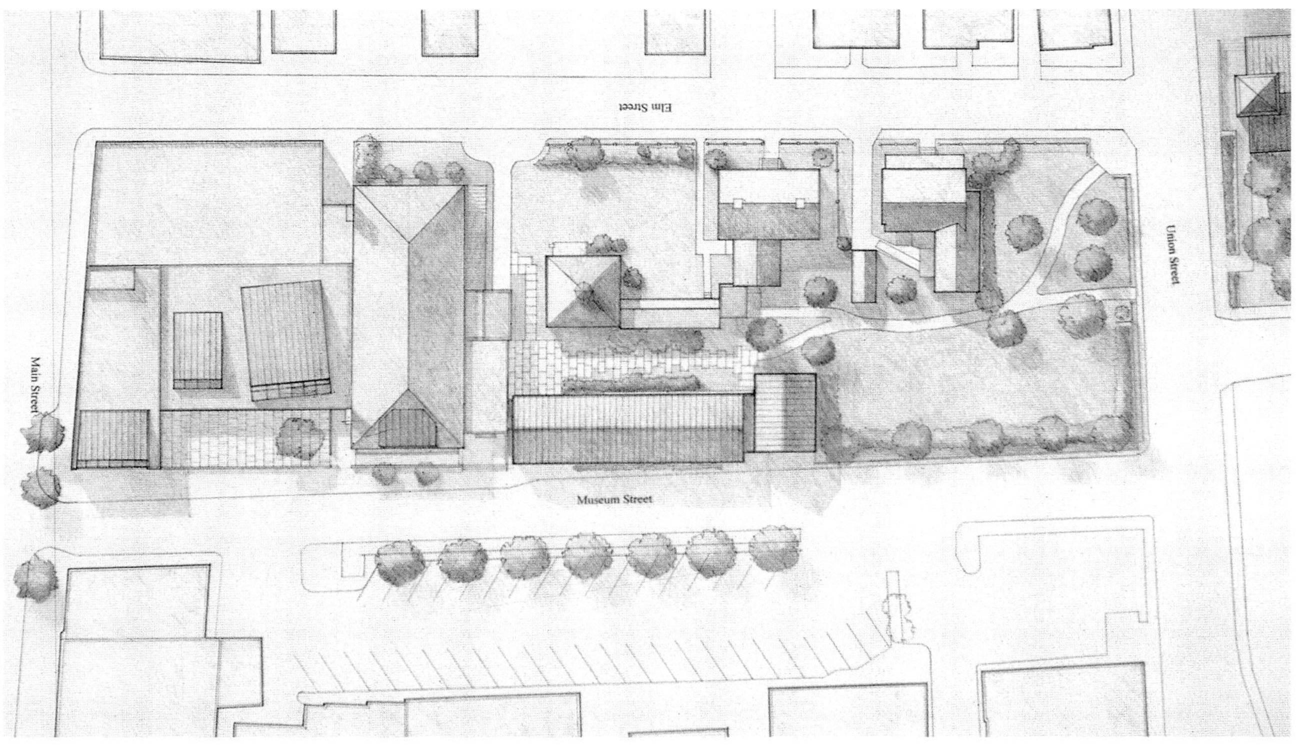

Elevations of the museum campus.

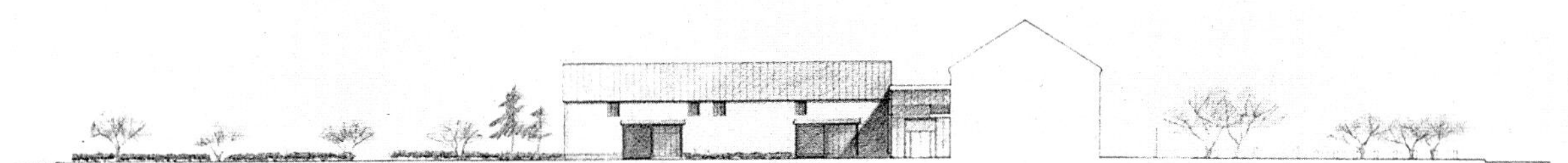

Entry to the museum complex on Museum Street.

View of entrance lobby.

Interior of the new Wyeth Study Center.

Stair landing at second floor of Wyeth Center galleries.

Below, views of stair to upper level gallery. Bottom, lower level gallery.

Model of upper level gallery with moveable panel system.

St. John's University Admissions Building

Jamaica, NY, 1997

St. John's University has the largest enrollment of any Catholic college in the USA, yet all of its students commute from around the New York City area. In an effort to attract students from all over the world, the university has now undertaken a major building campaign to add residence halls, parking garages, a new student center, a large chapel, classroom buildings, and a new admissions building.

Schwartz/Silver's task in designing the admissions building is to provide a new front door for the university. The site is located at the corner of the main quadrangle of the campus. Prospective students enter the building from a new courtyard and ascend up one floor to the level of the quadrangle, where the campus unfolds before them. On this upper level, an innovative digital resource center provides "one stop shopping" for all of the university's enrollment services.

The design of the building respects the language and materials of the adjacent 1950s buildings, while, at the same time, making a confidently modern statement that brings the campus up to date. Angled walls of glass, with expansive views across the main quadrangle, create a counterpoint to the more traditional facades of stone and brick with aluminum windows.

Client:
St. John's University
Master Plan Architect:
HLW International LLP
Structural Engineer:
LeMessurier Consultants
MEP Engineer:
R. G. Vanderweil Engineers, Inc.
Schwartz/Silver Project Team:
Warren Schwartz
Robert Silver
Mark Schatz
Scott Peltier
Anne Filson
Pamela Choi
Mimi Hoang

Opposite page, model, west elevation.

Below, study model,
looking southwest.
Bottom, detail of
vitreous insert
on study model.

Level 2
Resource Center.

Level 1
Reception Lobby.

Level 4.

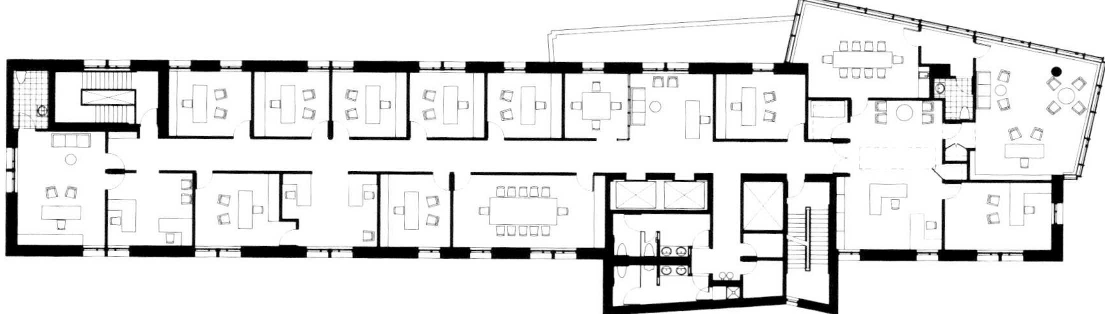

Level 3.

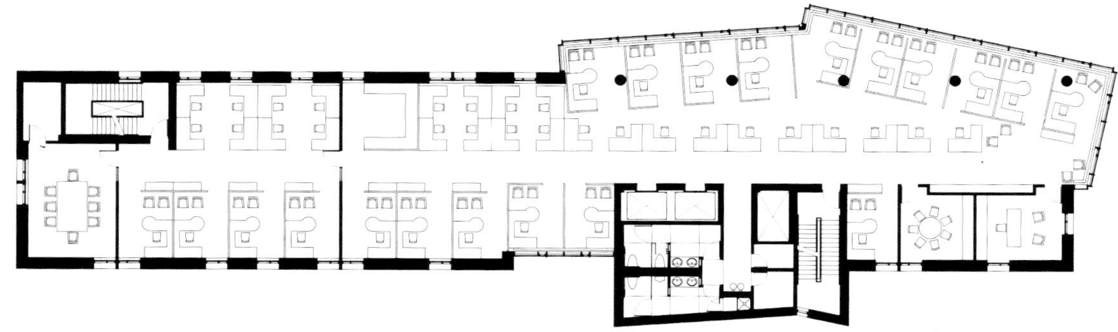

Level 2.

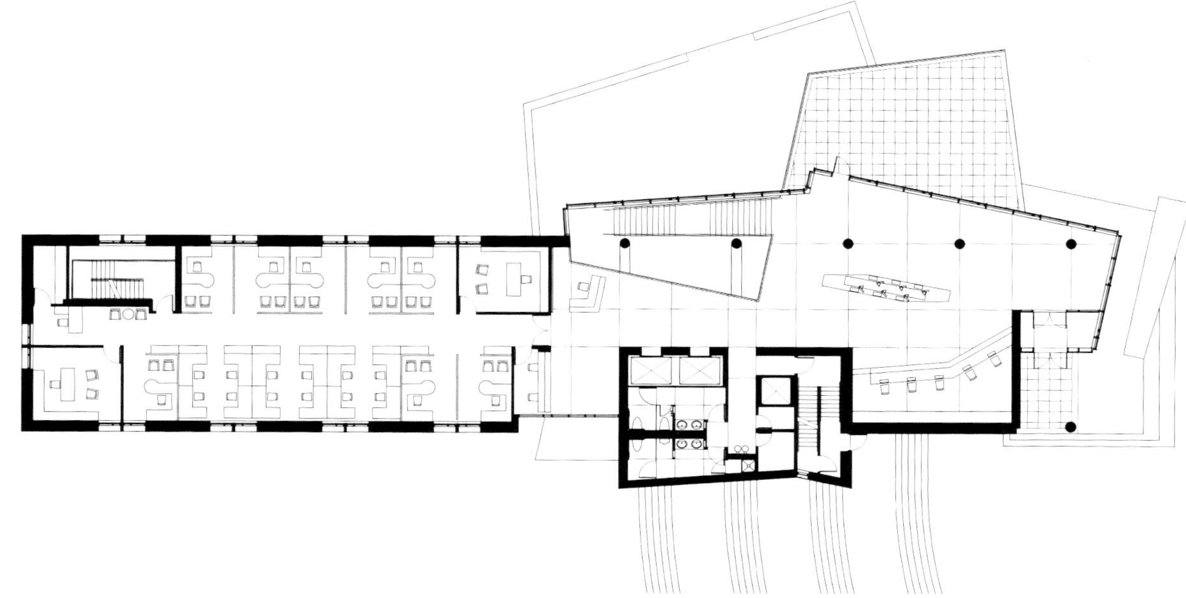

Level 1.

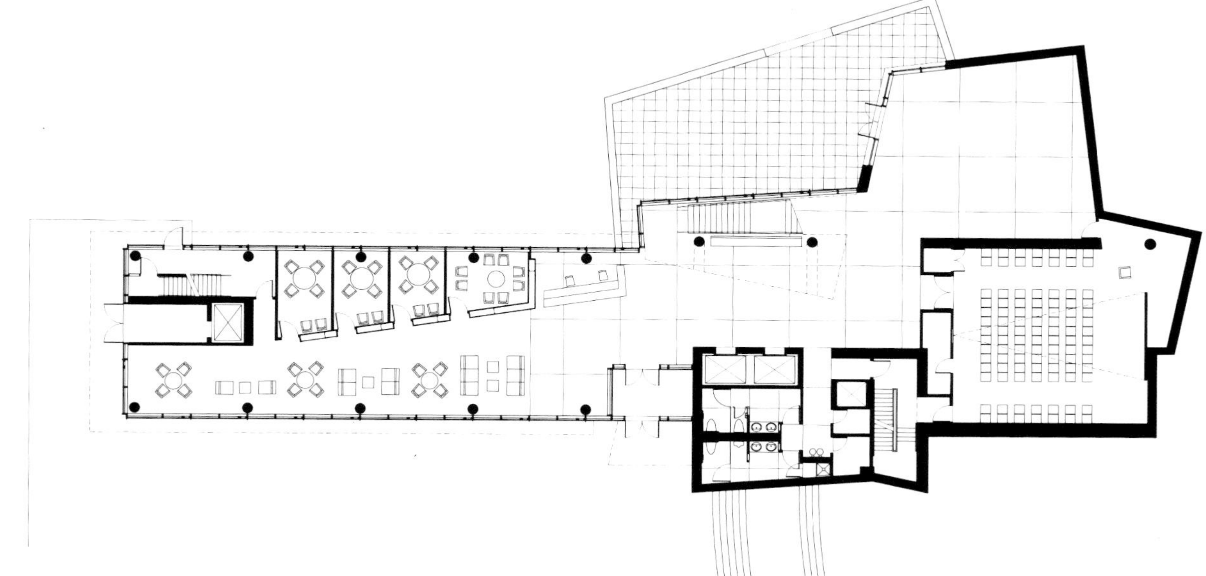

Below, study model, looking northwest. Bottom, detail of entry.

The Boston Athenaeum

Boston, MA, 1998-2001

Founded in 1807, the Boston Athenaeum is America's original independent library. The institution's energy and resources have spawned a number of key Boston cultural institutions, including the Museum of Fine Arts and the Museum of Science. Today its library collections comprise over half a million volumes, including George Washington's personal library. Its significant fine arts collections include paintings, prints, furniture and sculpture.

The Athenaeum's five-story building at 10 1/2 Beacon Street is an accretion of several transformations and additions over 150 years. Distinctions between these interventions, which must have been striking in their time, to modern eyes are clouded into an apparent unity. The last fundamental renovation of the building occurred in 1913, and introduced innovative uses of steel and glass into nineteenth century neo-classical spaces. Schwartz/Silver's design strategy for the current renovation and expansion is to allow the distinctions to re-emerge. The continuing history of the institution is supported with a further layer of invention – one discreet enough not to detract from its antecedents.

The newly expanded Athenaeum will be more open to the public, with the entry and first floor re-planned to accommodate events and exhibitions previously inaccessible in library areas. Other floors will undergo renovation to allow improved handling and storage of rare books, computerization of library catalogs, new facilities for visiting scholars, and consolidation of library staff areas. New space in a neighboring building will accommodate a larger and improved conservation lab, compact storage, and expanded service areas.

Client:
The Boston Athenaeum
Structural Engineer:
LeMessurier Consultants
MEP Engineer:
TMP Consulting Engineers, Inc.
Conservation Programming:
Garrison / Lull, Inc.
Civil Engineer:
Judith Nitsch Engineering, Inc.
Building Envelope:
Simpson Gumpertz & Heger, Inc.
Historic Preservation:
Preservation Technology Associates
Acoustic Consultant:
Cavanaugh Tocci Associates
Construction Manager:
Barr & Barr, Inc.
Archive Photograph:
Boston Athenaeum
Model Photograph:
Woodruff/Brown
Schwartz/Silver Project Team:
Robert Miklos
Robert Silver
Randolph Meiklejohn
Nelson Liu
Christopher Stanley
Sandra Saccone
Kristin Simonson
Steven Gerrard
Philip Chen
Michael Price
Matthew Littell
Wendy Cronk
Brian Mulder
Christopher Ingersoll
Melissa Braisted

Boston Athenaeum,
Beacon Street facade, 1902.
Oppsite page, 2nd floor
Bow Room before renovation.

North-South section.

First floor
before renovation.

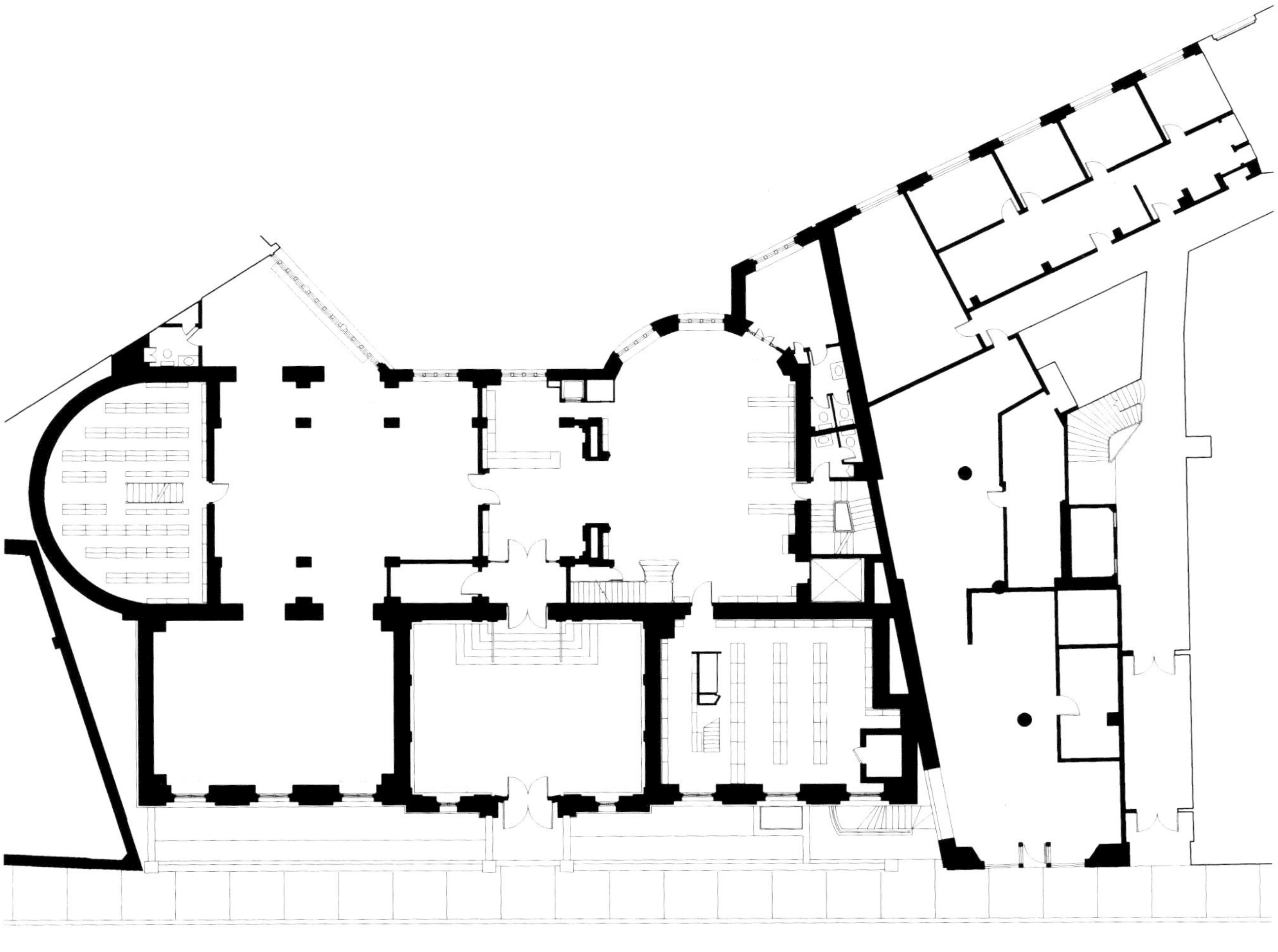

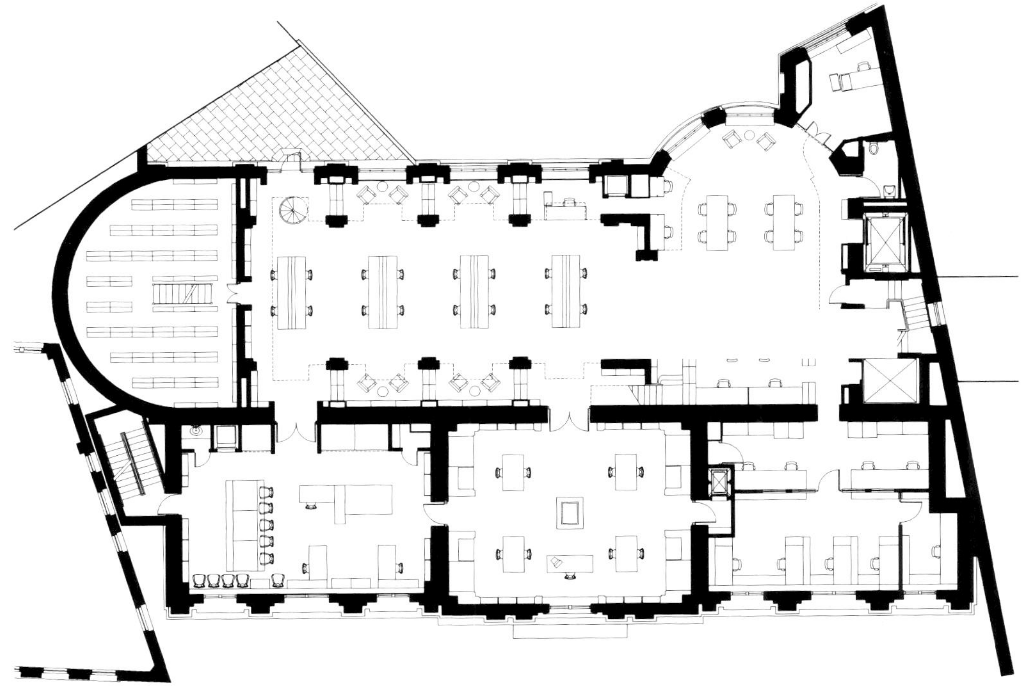

Second floor
after renovation.

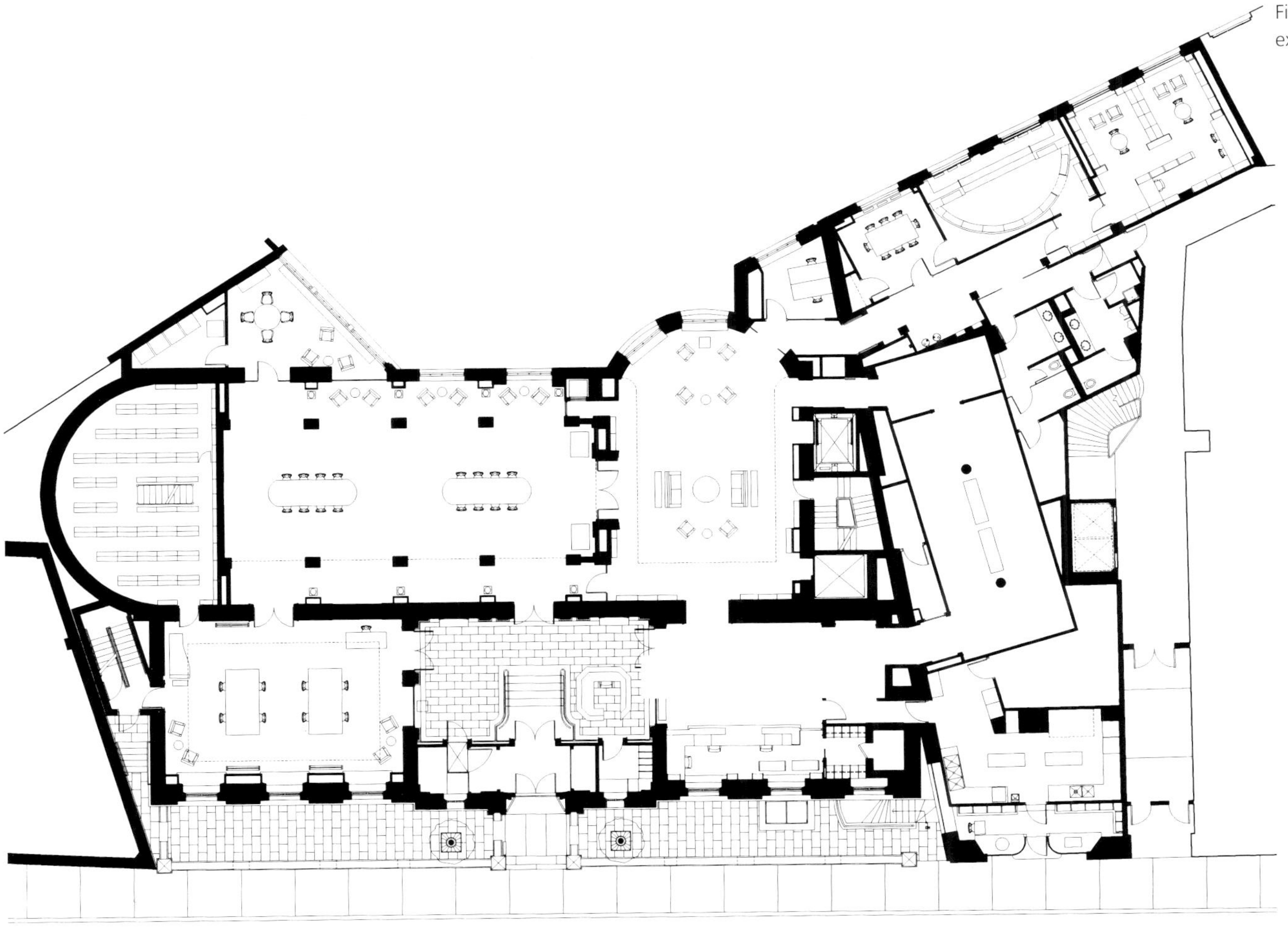

First floor after
expansion/renovation.

Below, first floor
Long Room
before renovation.
Bottom left, Bow
Room, first floor.
Bottom right, Special
Collections Room.

Presentation model
of first floor.

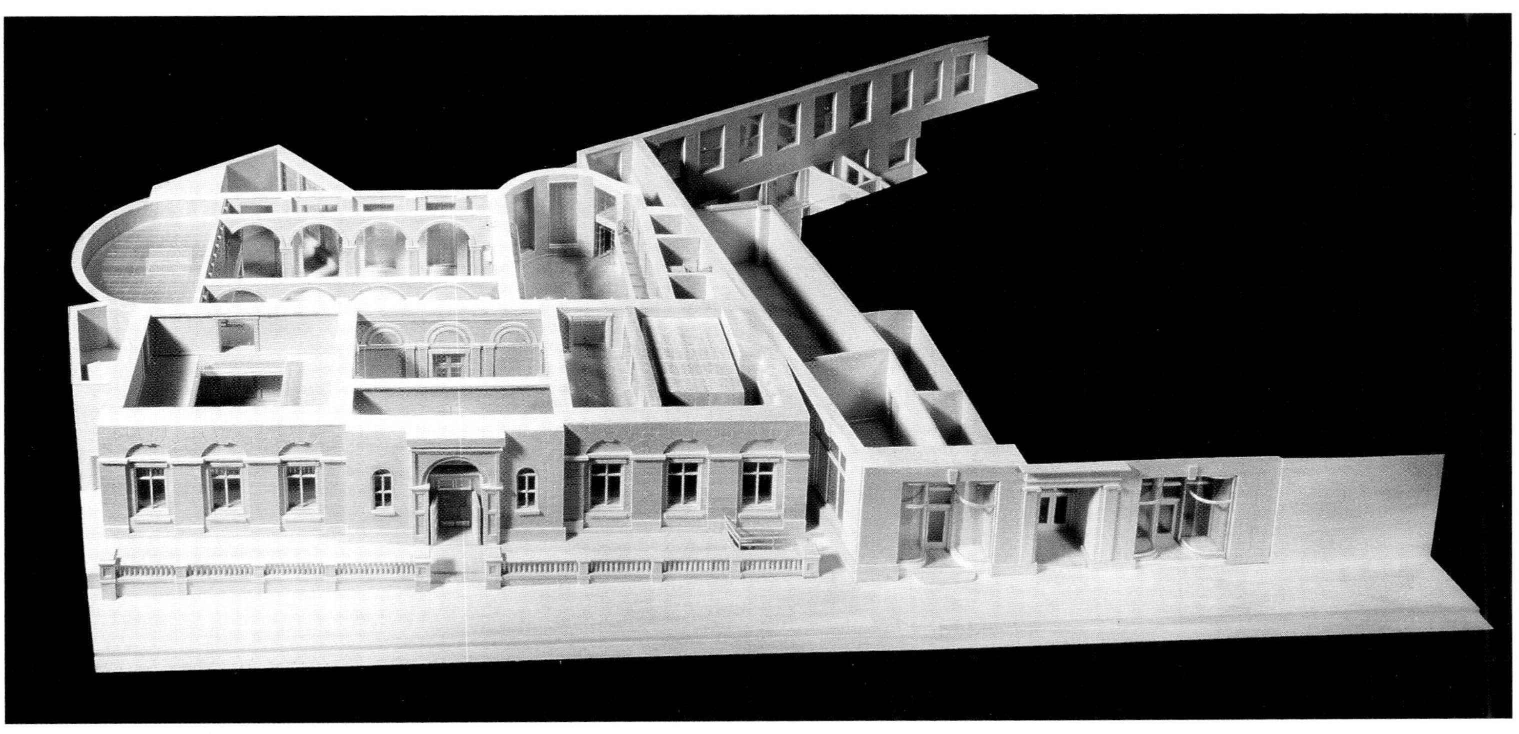

Ames Free Library

North Easton, MA, 1998-2001

Designed by H. H. Richardson in 1877-1879, this library was the first of five projects by the architect commissioned by the Ames family for the town of North Easton. Highly celebrated as one of his best works, it was in many ways the prototype for the American town library. The children's wing, built in 1931, has been the only significant addition to the facility, and was discreetly placed to the rear so that the original effect of the main aspect of the building could remain intact. The building is so revered that past attempts to expand the library, to keep up with modern-day needs, became mired in controversy and were abandoned. The dilemma was whether to prioritize the library's functional purpose as a social facility in the town, or whether to preserve it as a historic relic.

Schwartz/Silver's design strategy is conceived to address both needs at once: a living, functional facility that makes a distinctive feature of its past heritage. The overcrowded reading room will be relieved by new spaces for book stacks, administrative uses and meeting rooms — which will more than double the size of the library. Interior spaces in the Richardson building will be restored to their original character with period fixtures and furnishings. As with the 1931 addition, new construction will all be discreetly created behind the original building. Much of the new program will be integrated into the sloping topography of the site, organized around a lower level courtyard. This develops the landscape as a feature of the library in a way that that had not been possible for Richardson (despite his association with Olmsted for several other projects in the town). The various forms of the addition are designed to establish a connection with the wall structures of an adjacent historic garden, which was acquired to extend the site of the library. They do not mimic the style of the original building but, in a quietly deferential manner, throw its historic character into relief. Where they are above grade, these structures are subsidiary in their presence, like garden outbuildings.

Client:
Ames Free Library/Easton's Public Library
Associated Architect:
Albert, Righter, & Tittman Architects, Inc.
Structural Engineer:
LeMessurier Consultants
MEP Engineer:
TMP Consulting Engineers, Inc.
Civil Engineering:
Judith Nitsch Engineering, Inc.
Historic Preservation:
Preservation Technology Associates
Landscape:
Richard Burck Associates
Schwartz/Silver Project Team:
Robert Miklos
Angela Ward Hyatt
Scott Tulay
Peter Kleiner
Christopher Ingersoll
Stephen Davis
Robert Silver

Opposite page, aerial view of study model, showing library and neighboring Oakes Ames Memorial Hall.
Left, the library's Main Street facade, 1883.

View from Main Street, showing neighboring Oakes Ames Memorial Hall.

New entry
from garden.

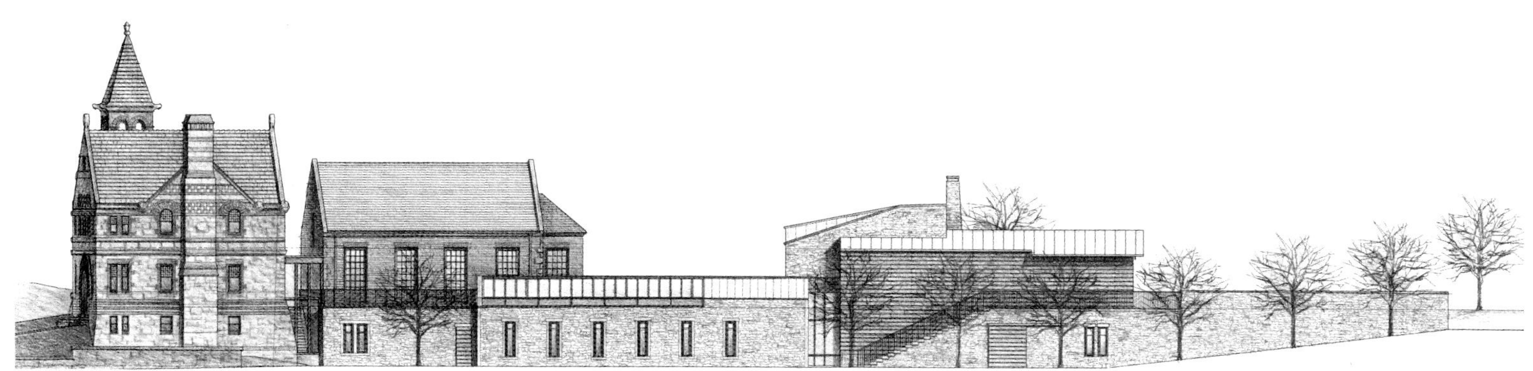

North elevation.

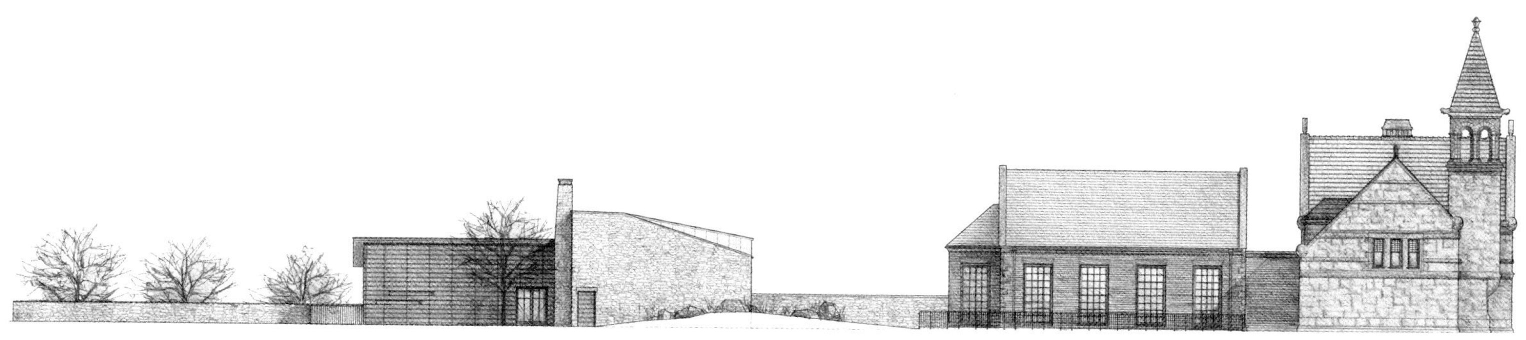

South elevation.

West elevation.

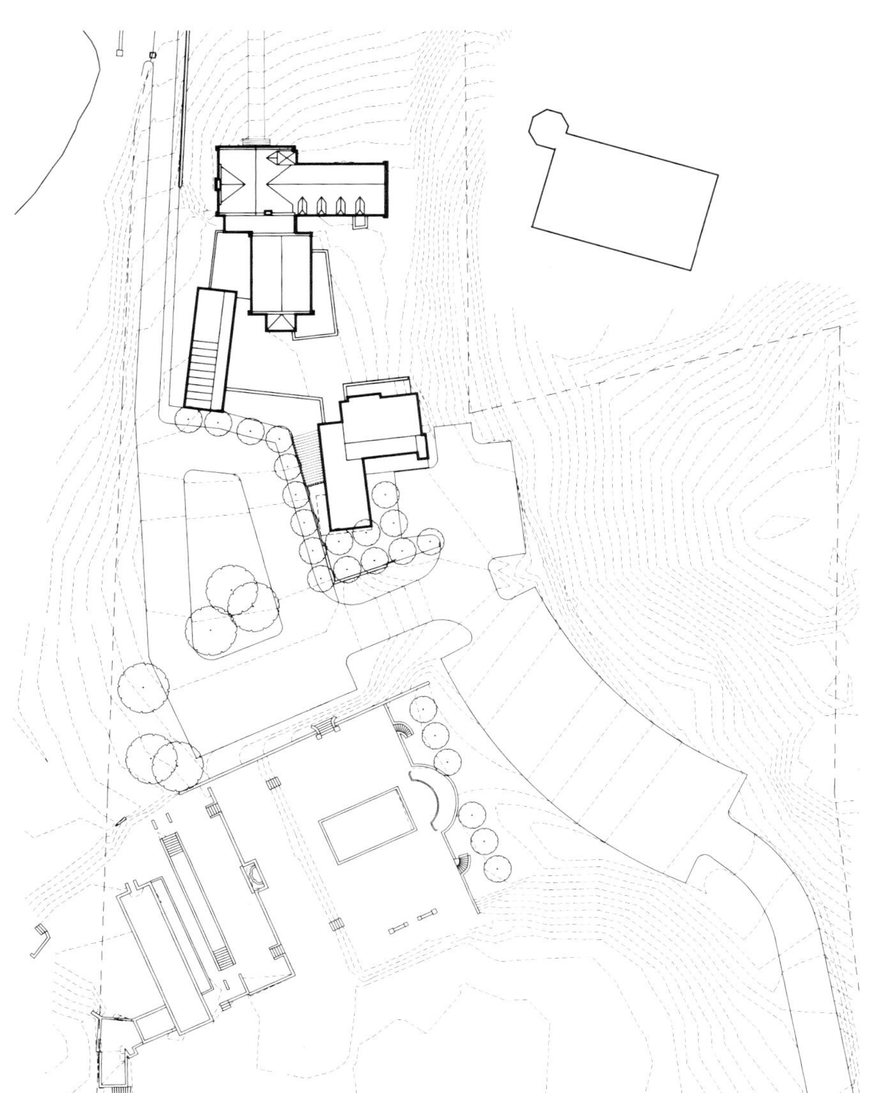

Left, site plan, showing historic Queset Garden walls. Bottom, Level 0 and Level 1.

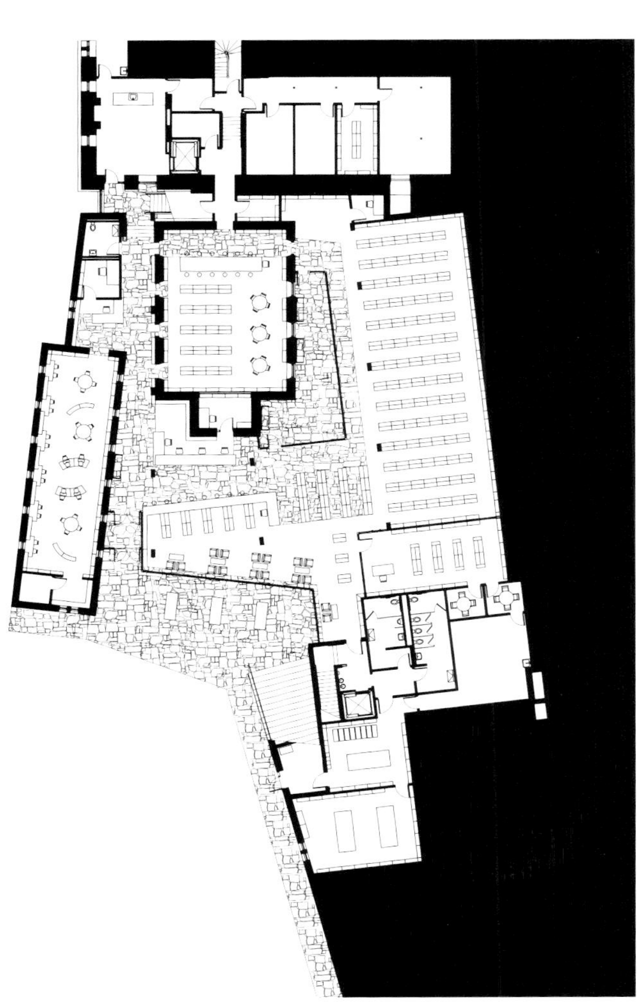

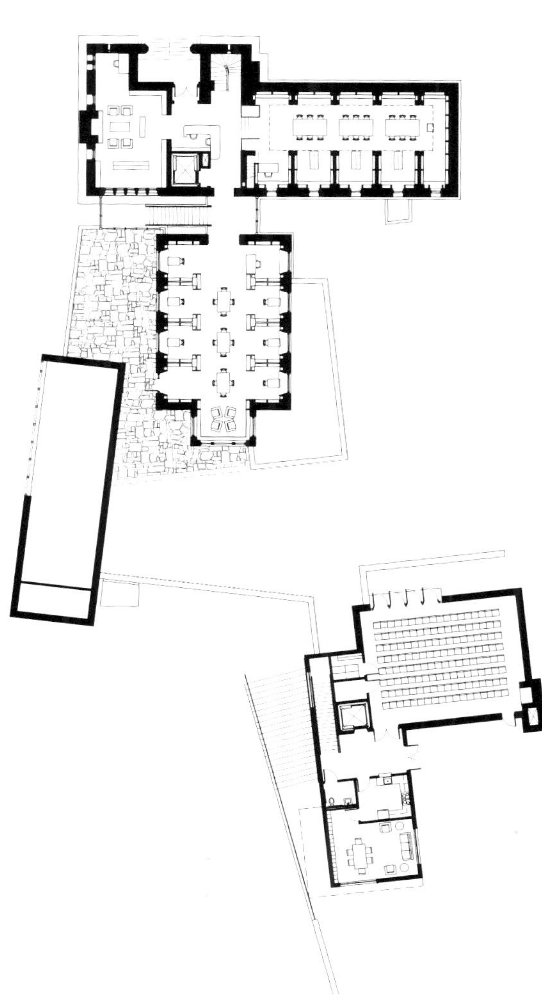

Louisiana State University Museum of Art

Baton Rouge, LA, 1998-1999

The LSU Museum of Art has long been a modest collection in small quarters on the university campus. In considering the need for expansion, a decision was made to reconceptualize the museum on a much larger scale. The university wanted to signal a commitment to the arts as an essential part of its life and identity. Because of LSU's location in Baton Rouge, the capital of Louisiana, and a perceived lack of such cultural attractions in the region, the project swiftly gathered momentum in the broader community. The issue of the design of the building, and what it might reflect or represent about the state as a whole, then became the focus of a stakeholder group that had broadened far beyond LSU.

Extending the terms of the debate beyond the stereotype of the Southern Plantation building, Schwartz/Silver's approach draws upon the full range of creative adaptation and combination of influences that can be found in the architectural heritage of the state, from "Shotgun" and "Dog-Trot" houses to agrarian structures. All of these various hybrids are responses to the Louisiana climate, where the need for shade and rain protection is primary. A vast canopy shades the entire building on its south and west sides, together with a pergola that extends out to provide additional shade across the terrace. The elongation of the building, combined with these canopies, provides an image for the museum that relates to the characteristic porches of the plantations while respecting a variety of other local traditions as well. A relationship is established to the Italianate architecture of the LSU campus, where the buildings are raised on plinths, by the monumental terrace on which the museum sits. This elevates the building in its open parkland site, on the outskirts of Baton Rouge. As visitors approach the museum, they ascend terraced steps up to the building. Once inside, they ascend the grand interior stairway leading up to the galleries. The experience gives a literal and metaphorical dimension to the goal of elevating the arts.

Client:
Louisiana State University
Associated Architect:
Post Architects
Museum Consultant:
John L. Hilberry & Associates
Structural Engineer:
McKee & Deville Consulting Engineers
MEP Engineer:
George W. Tucker & Associates
Civil Engineer:
Ferris Engineering & Surveying
Schwartz/Silver Project team:
Warren Schwartz
Christopher Ingersoll
Philip Chen
Steven Gerrard

Opposite page, south facade.

Level 3.

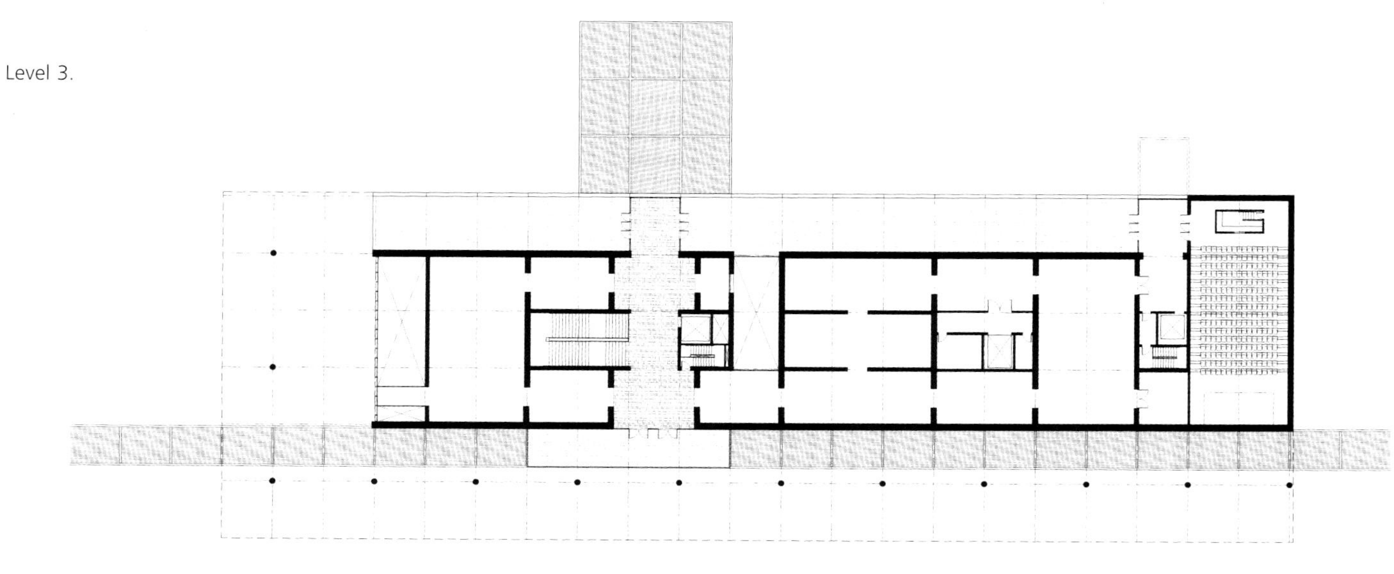

Level 2.

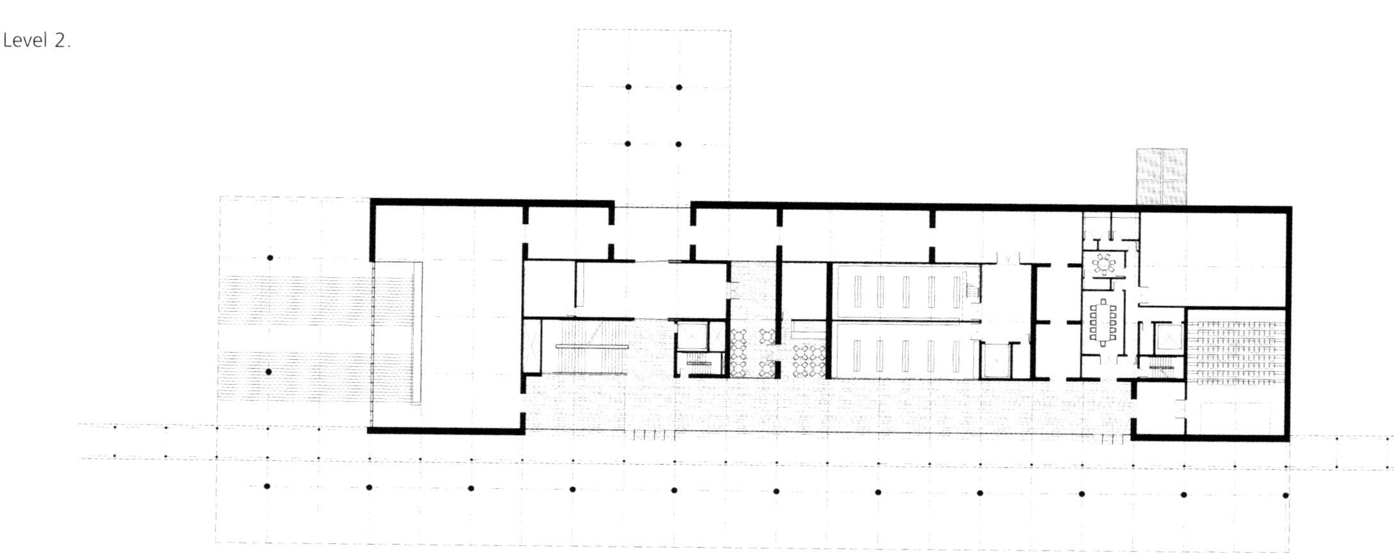

Level 1.

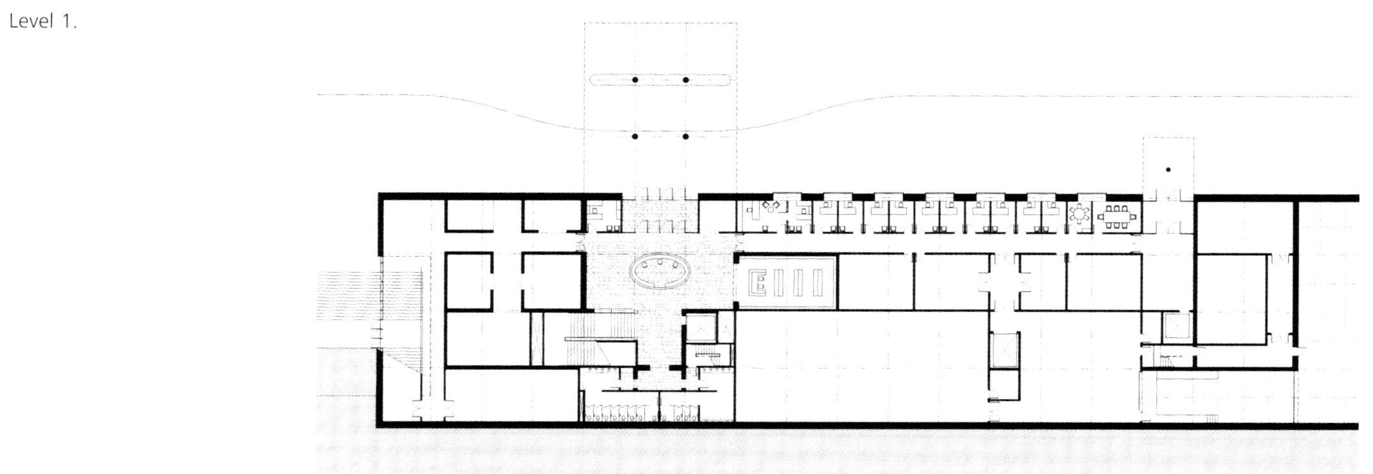

From top, north, south and west elevations.

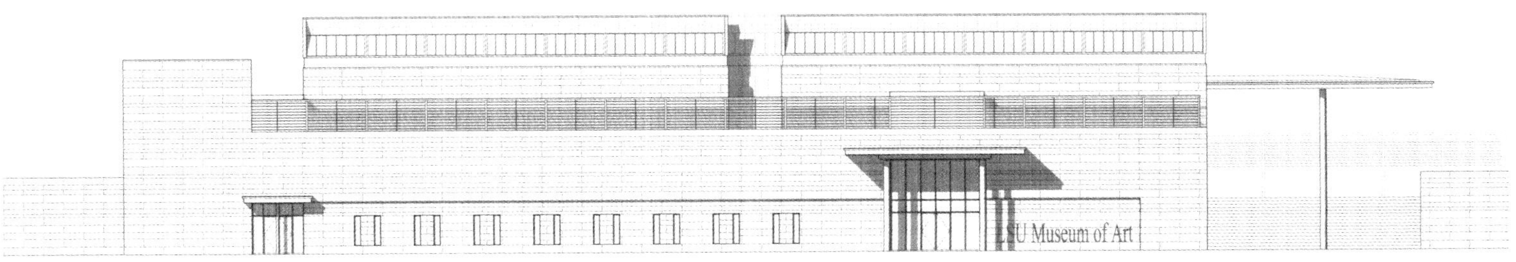

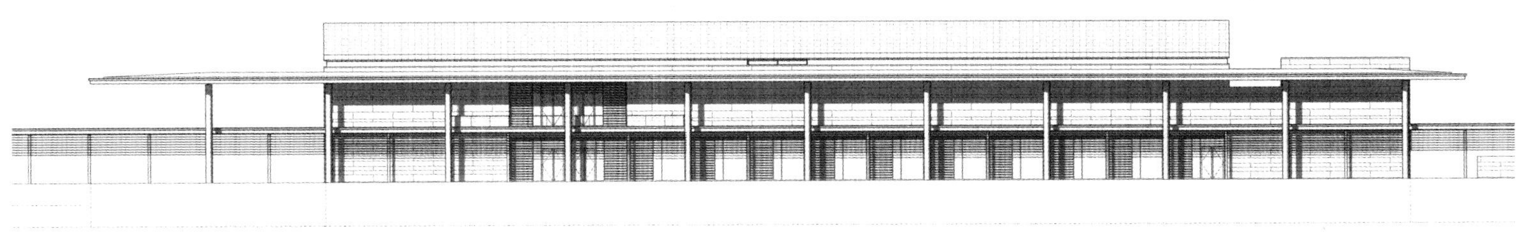

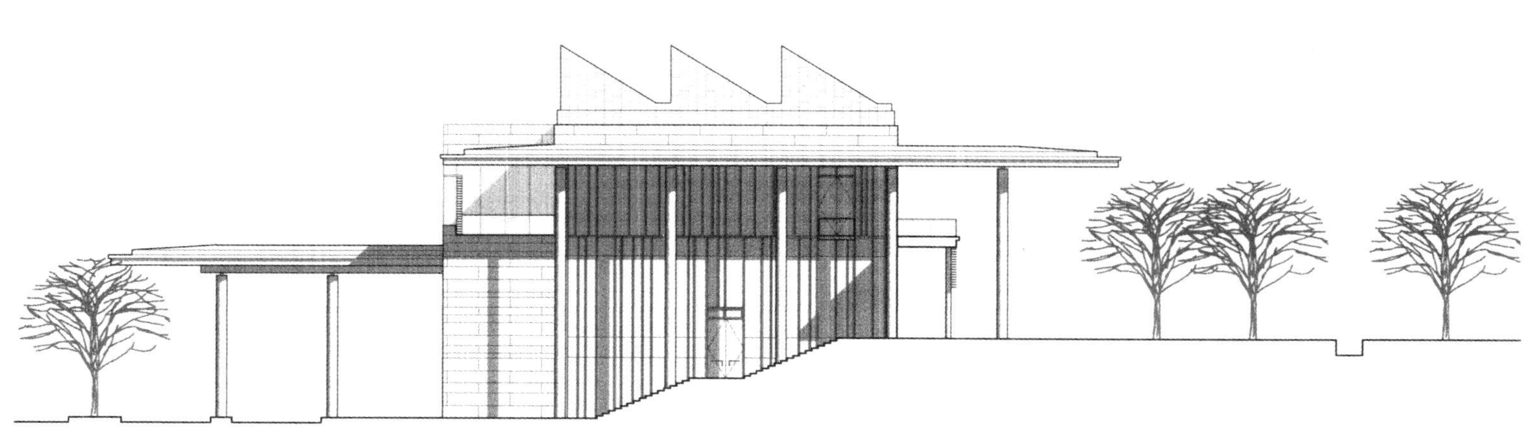

Study model, aerial view looking southeast.

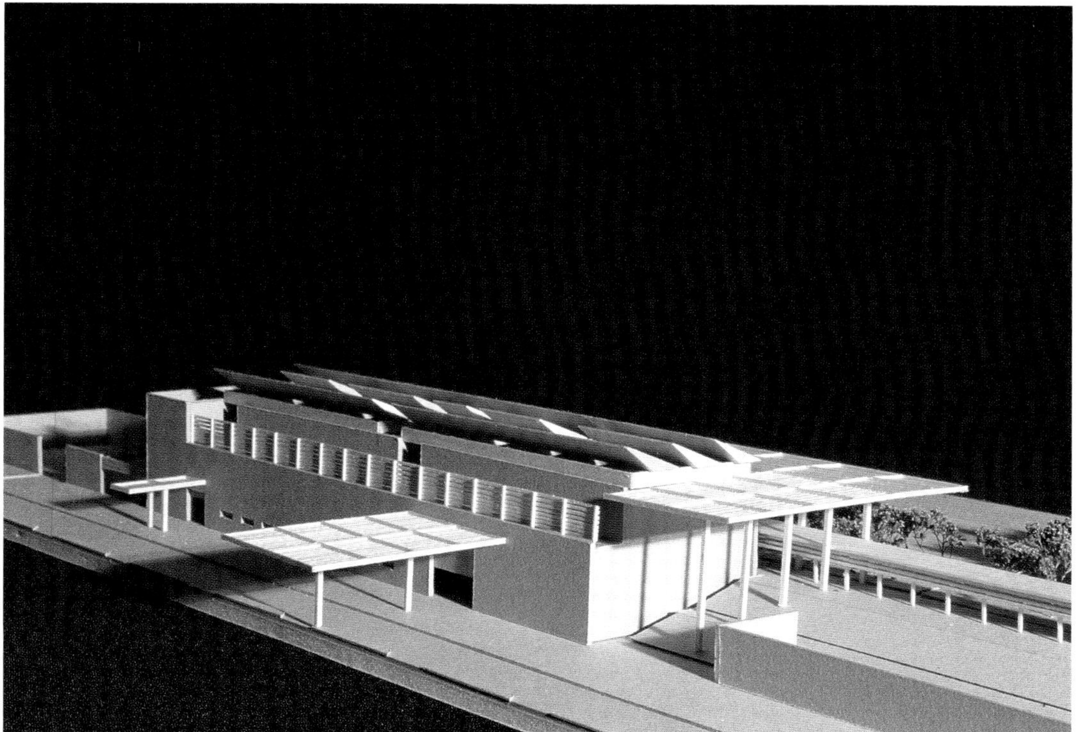

Study model, aerial view looking southwest.

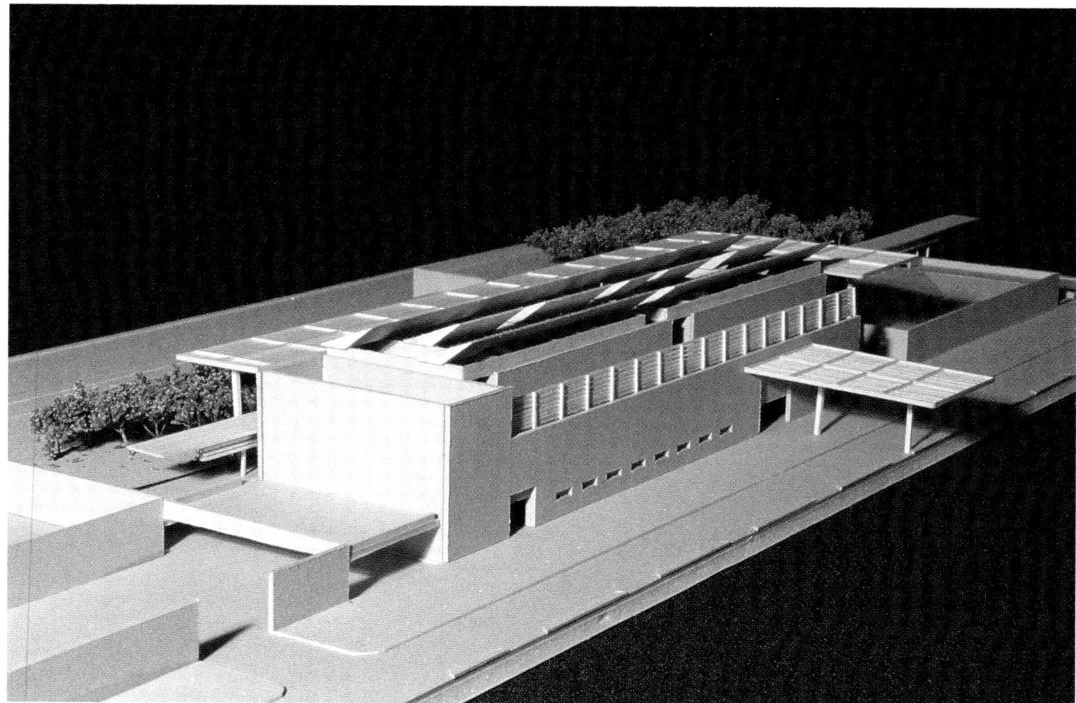

Study model, aerial view looking northwest.

Views of interior spaces.

ica

Institute of Contemporary Art

Boston, MA, 1999

Client:
Institute of Contemporary Art
Schwartz/Silver Project Team:
Warren Schwartz
Mark Schatz
Pamela Choi

Established in Boston at the same time as the Museum of Modern Art in New York, the ICA has, until recently, not developed a substantial presence in the cultural life of the city. However, an opportunity to do so occurred in 1999 when the City of Boston required the construction of a major cultural facility as part of the commercial development of its downtown seaport district. In order to make a convincing case to the city and the developers that the ICA would be the best contender for this civic role, Schwartz/Silver was commissioned to develop a building design that would explain the potential of the new museum for Boston.

Unlike many art museums, the 60,000 square foot building is transparent, so that it can provide constant animation for the waterfront district. The elevator shafts and core mechanical systems are located on the two street edges to allow maximum transparency on the waterfront facades and through the roof. Similarly, offices and other amenities are integrated to form a horizontally striated outer wall on the southeastern side and clear space for larger program elements in the central area of the building. The slope of the auditorium in the 400-seat theater provides a distinctively shaped volume that hangs inside the main space. Other hanging volumes visible from outside are galleries for exhibits that require controlled lighting conditions. The passage of visitors up stairways to these various spaces activates the building. The oversized shafts that protrude out of the rooftop sculpture garden provide modulated daylight for the galleries and performance space. After dark they project light into the night sky.

Opposite page, view from harbor by night.

Site plans of Fan
Pier development.

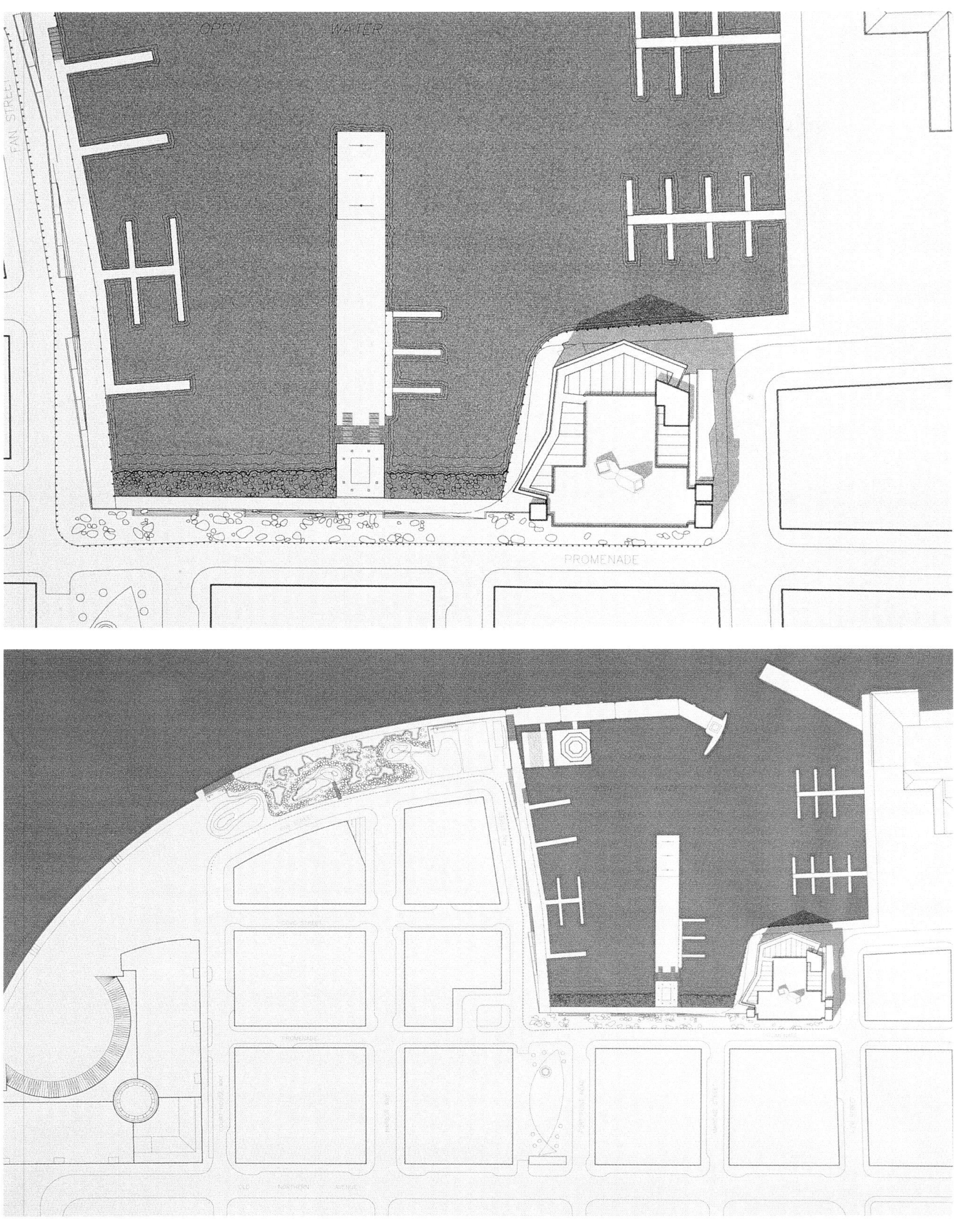

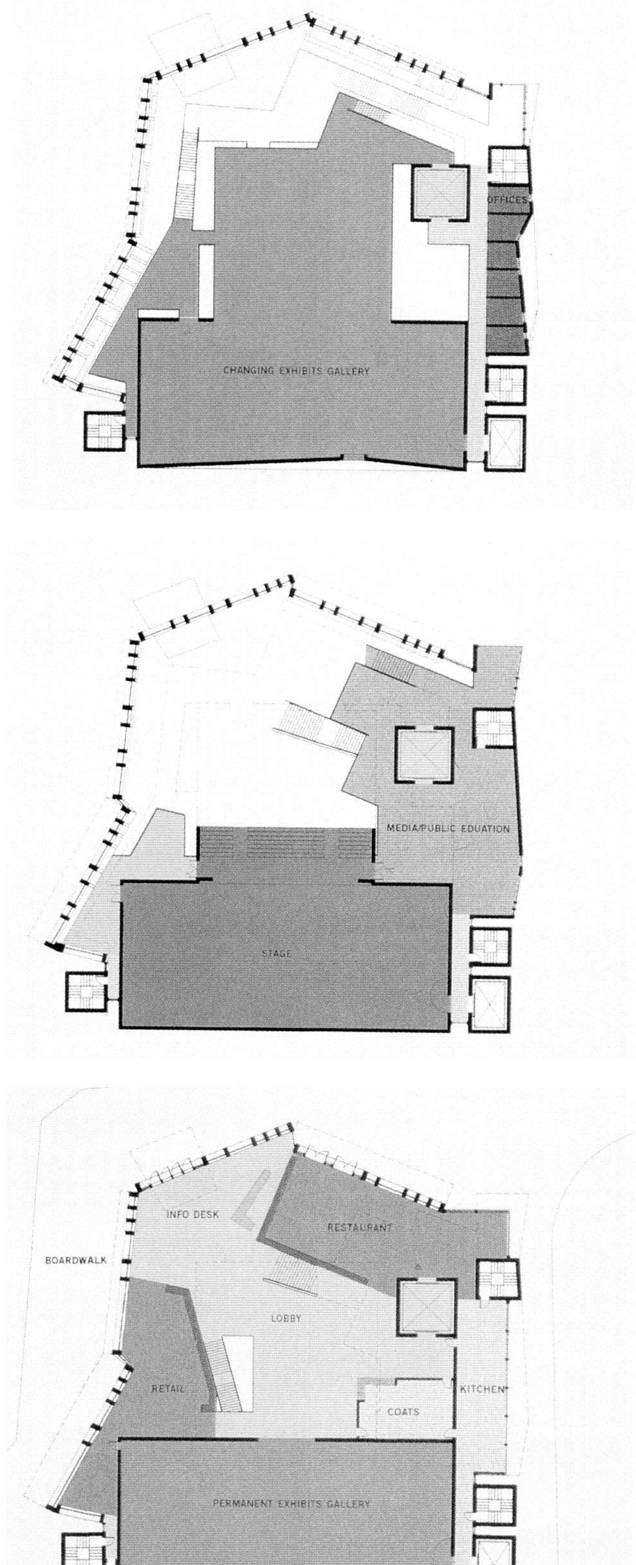

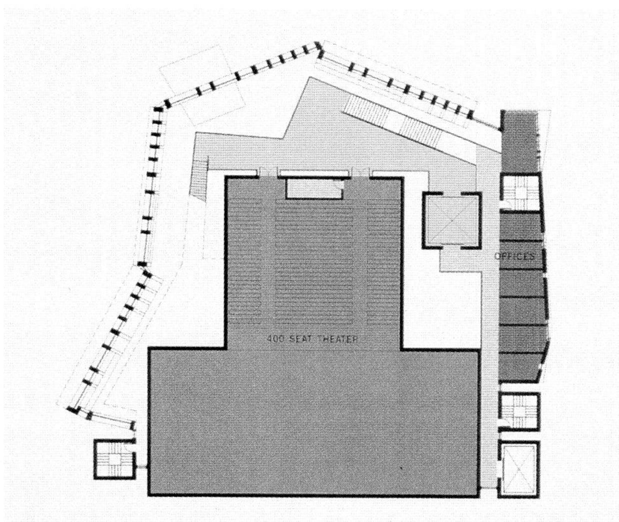

Left, from top, levels 4, 2 and 1. Right, from top, sculpture terrace level and level 3.

Below, sketch of view from second level balcony. Bottom, study model view looking northeast.

Below, study model view from north. Bottom, study model view looking southwest.

Abbe Museum

Bar Harbor, ME, 1997-2001

The Abbe Museum, with its collections of Native American artifacts, has been an important part of Maine's cultural landscape since it was founded in 1928. It is still located in its original trailside building in Acadia National Park. This project will create a second location for the institution in the more populous setting of Bar Harbor. The site includes an 1890s Shingle Style building, an example of the local architectural heritage, which is being adapted and expanded for the new museum. The principal addition is for a double height exhibit gallery. It continues the forms and materials of the original building on the other side of a small open courtyard for outdoors events. A second addition leading off the main building has a markedly different character, a small tower in the form of a rotated ellipse. The Abbe includes collections and programs of the living history of the Maliseet, Micmac, Passamaquoddy and Penobscot peoples – the four federally recognized Native American tribes in Maine. This suggested the need for a building that would speak to the presence of these cultural traditions within the existing heritage of Bar Harbor. The design of the circular tower was the outcome of a series of discussions with Maine Native Americans to create an appropriate space for various special events and activities. The details of construction and finish are drawn from techniques used in making canoes, baskets and other vessels. It presents a distinctive counterpoint to the rectilinear volumes of surrounding buildings without disrespecting the character of the context. It is an unusual and intriguing form designed to draw the curiosity of visitors and identify the museum with an iconic landmark.

Client:
Abbe Museum
Structural & MEP Engineer:
Lanpher Associates Inc.
Landscape Architect:
Coplon Associates
Civil Engineer:
Bruce Crawford & Co.
Contractor:
E.L. Shea, Inc.
Building Envelope:
Simpson, Gumpertz & Heger
Schwartz/Silver Project Team:
Jonathan Traficonte
Robert Miklos
Warren Schwartz
Robert Silver
Stephen Davis
Pamela Choi
Matthew Littell
Steven Gerrard
Scott Peltier

Opposite page, model of Museum campus looking north on School Street.

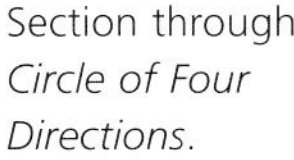

Section through *Circle of Four Directions*.

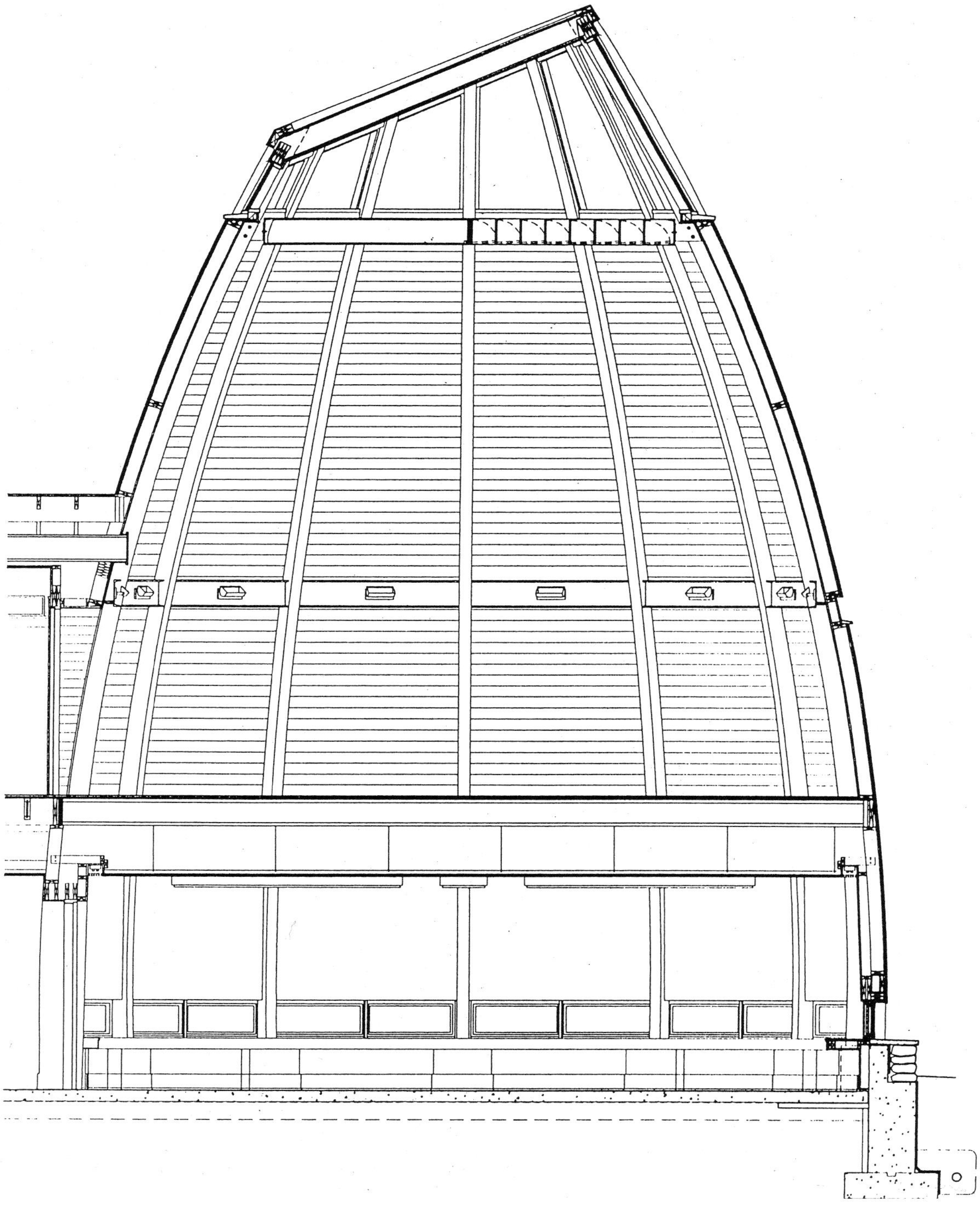

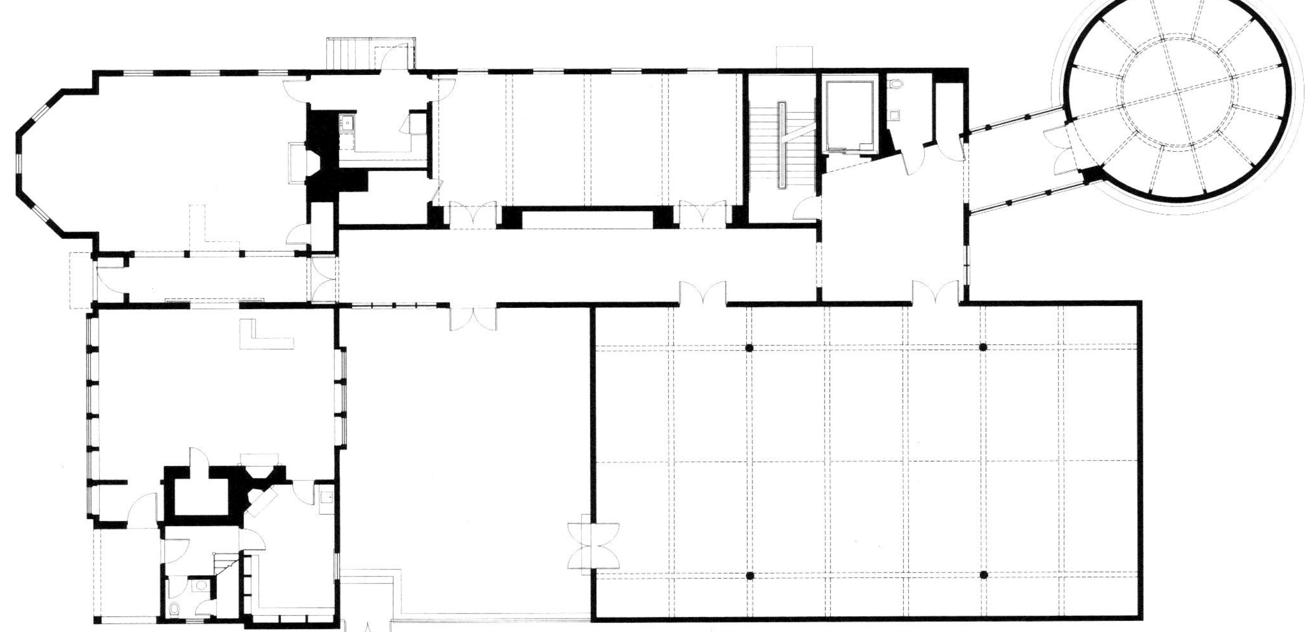

Plan of ground floor.

Aerial view of campus model.

Model of *Circle of Four Directions.*

Davoli-McDonagh Residence

Lincoln, MA, 1999-2001

Lincoln is an area of suburban Boston where the landscape has been carefully preserved in its nineteenth century agrarian condition. It still has working farms, open fields bounded by dry-stone walls, and uncultivated woods. The five-acre site of this house is in a wooded area, sharply sloping down to a pond.

In designing the house, it was a priority to respect the attributes of the existing landscape: the rolling topography, the trees, forest ground cover, and pond. The drive up to the house follows an existing clearing in the site and, on arrival, allows access to a garage hidden in the landscape. Facing the entry is a stone court, informally accommodating guest parking between trees. The overall form of the building is of a loop, which wraps around an internal courtyard. The upper end of the loop, cantilevered over the entrance, moves down to follow the curve of the land until it curls into the slope. This spiraling form allows the interior spaces to be arranged for optimum views of the surroundings, particularly across to the pond. Seen through large areas of glass delineated by slate walls, these views articulate the spaces inside without any need for formal compartmentalization. Interior and exterior flow into one another, integrating the building into the landscape.

The owners of the house, an energetic executive and a university professor with grown children, both have varied interests and enjoy working and entertaining at home. The idiosyncratic non-conformism underpinning the design is a function of their own passionate commitment to thoughtful innovation in all their various fields of interest.

Clients:
Robert Davoli, Eileen McDonagh
Structural Engineer:
LeMessurier Consultants
HVAC Engineer:
Sun Engineering
Electrical/Plumbing Engineer:
Eric Johnson Engineering and Design
Landscape Design:
Stephen Stimson Associates
Building Envelope:
Simpson, Gumpertz & Heger
Lighting Design:
Berg-Howland Associates
Contractor:
Thoughtforms Corporation
Schwartz/Silver Project Team:
Warren Schwartz
Steven Gerrard
Christopher Ingersoll
Michael Price
Paul Stanbridge
Robert Silver

Opposite page, view from entry drive.

Below, landscape site plan, showing interior and exterior flooring materials. Bottom, south elevation, showing main entry.

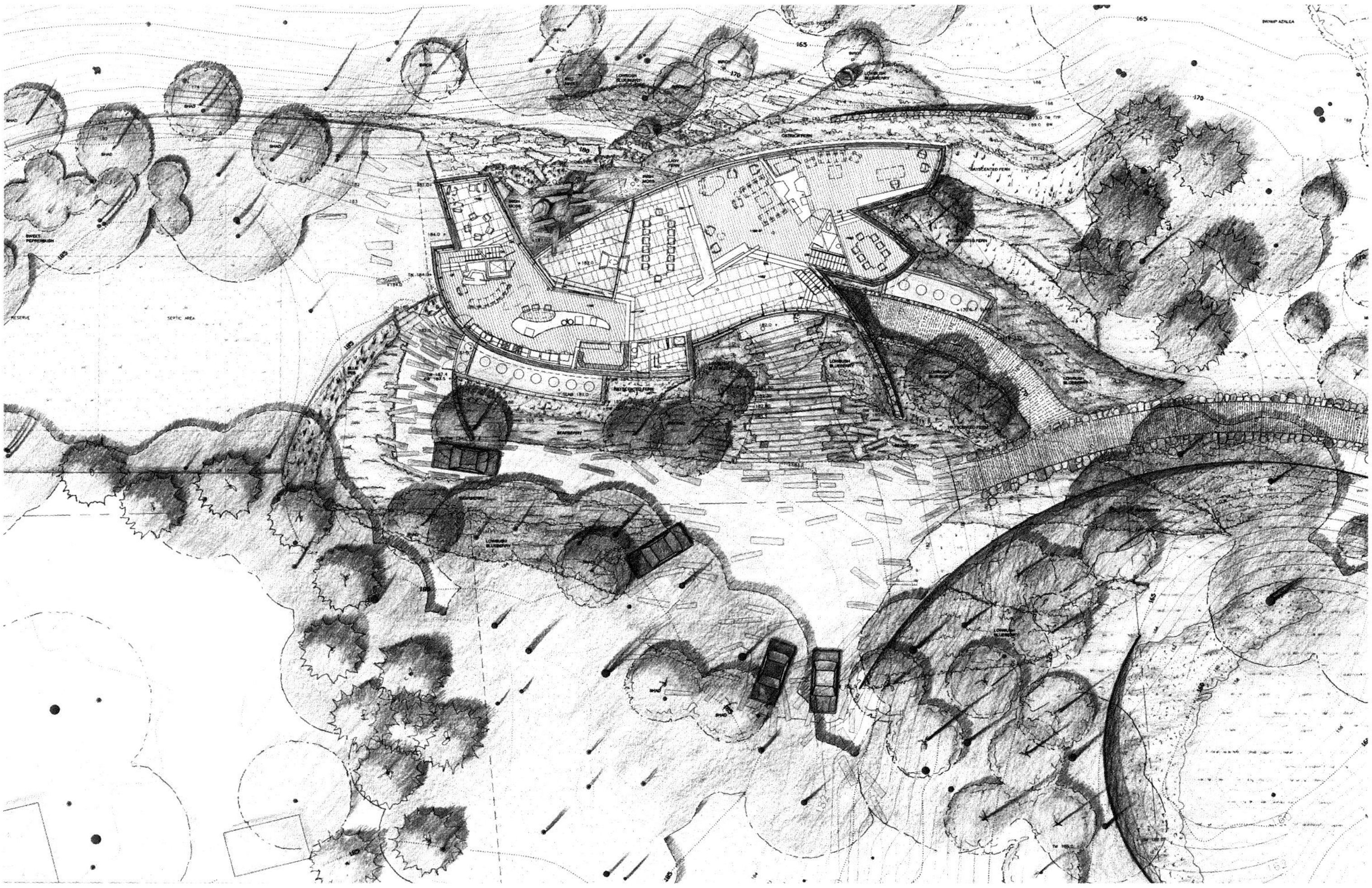

Level 3.

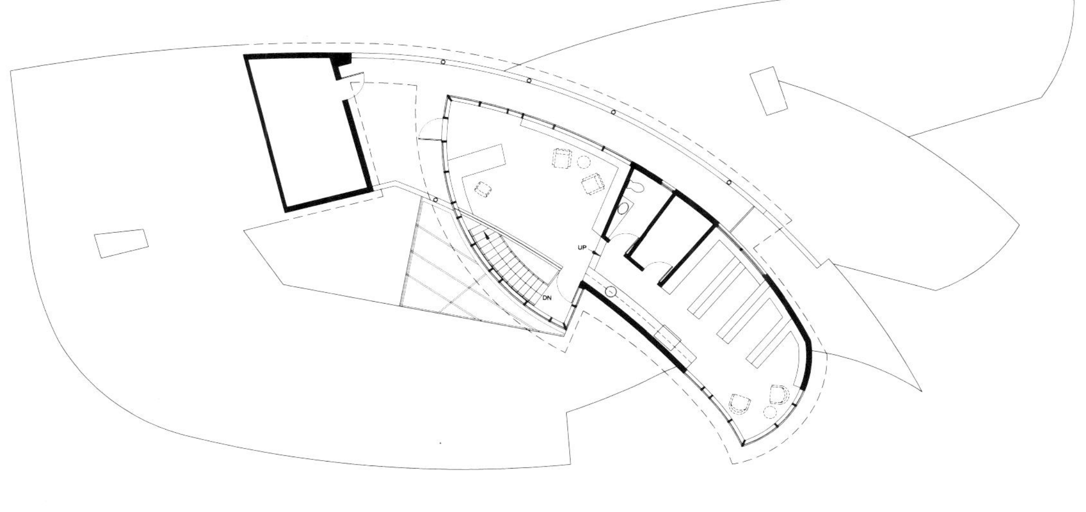

Level 2.

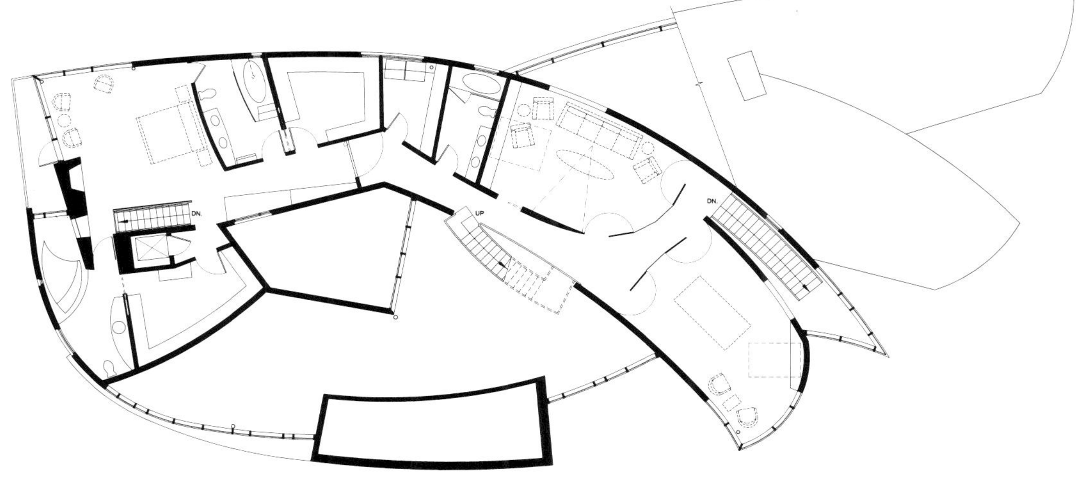

Level 1.

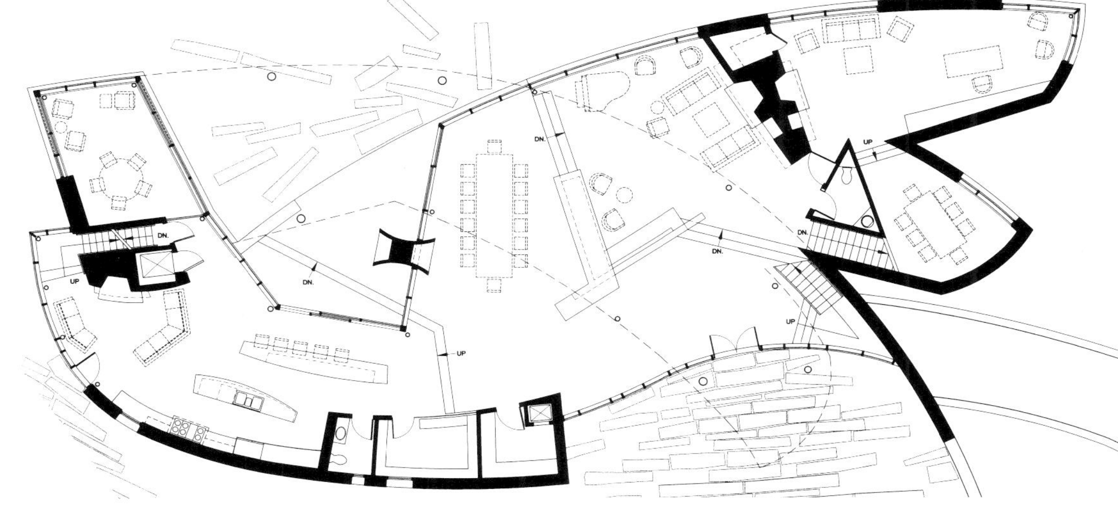

Level 0.

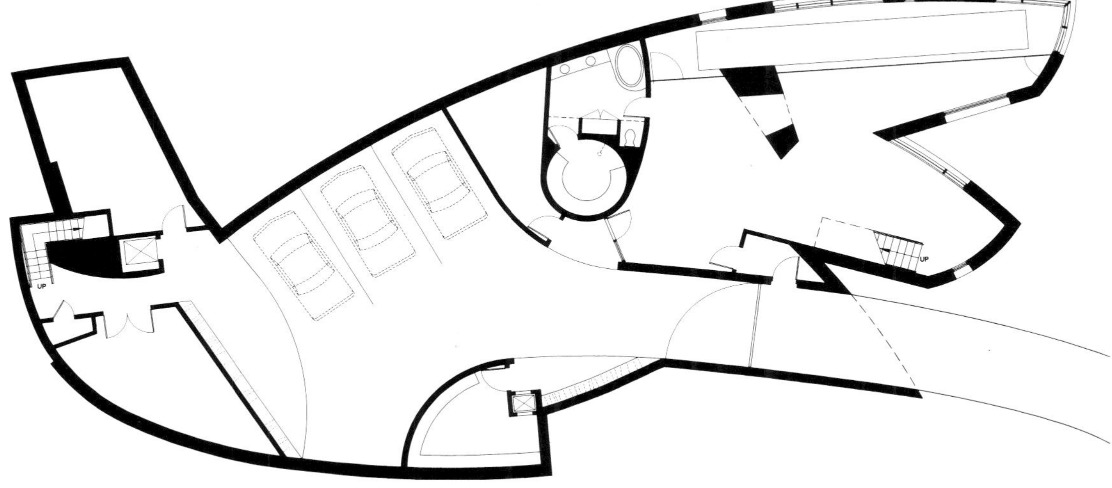

Below, computer
model of east
elevation.
Bottom, aerial view
from northwest.

Aerial view from northeast.

Below, level 1 view from kitchen through to main living area.
Bottom, level 1 view from entry area back through to kitchen and courtyard.

View of skylight
over dining area.

Awards

American Institute of Architects National Honor Awards

2000
Honor Award for Architecture:
Hyde Park Branch Library,
Boston, MA.

1994
Honor Award for Architecture:
Firehouse Arts Center, Newburyport, MA.

1993
National Library Award (with the American Library Association):
MIT Rotch Library of Art, Architecture and Planning,
Cambridge, MA.

1991
Honor Award for Architecture:
360 Newbury Street, Boston, MA
(with Frank O. Gehry & Associates, Design Architect).

1990
Honor Award for Architecture:
The House at Tanglewood,
West Stockbridge, MA.

American Institute of Architects Chapter Awards

2000
Design Award:
American Institute of Architects Pennsylvania Chapter:
Two Rivers Landing, Easton, PA
(with Wallace & Watson Associates, Executive Architects).

2000
Housing Design Award,
Boston Society of Architects/American Institute of Architects
New York Chapter:
Vacation House, Cape Cod, MA

2000
Young Architects' Award of the
Boston Society of Architects, Citation:
Abbe Museum, Bar Harbor, ME

2000
Young Architects' Award of the
Boston Society of Architects, Citation:
World Trade Center Marine Terminal, Boston, MA

1998
Young Architects' Award of the
Boston Society of Architects , Citation:
Candela Laserspa, Boston, MA.

1997
Award for Excellence in Architecture, Eastern Pennsylvania Chapter of the American Institute of Architects:
Two Rivers Landing, Easton, PA
(with Wallace & Watson Associates, Executive Architects).

1996
Honor Award,
Boston Society of Architects:
Two Rivers Landing, Easton, PA
(with Wallace & Watson Associates, Executive Architects).

1994
Merit Award,
Boston Society of Architects:
Proctor Academy Learning Center, Andover, NH.

1993
Harleston Parker Gold Medal
of the Boston Society of Architects
and the City of Boston:
MIT Rotch Library of Art, Architecture, and Planning,
Cambridge, MA.

1991
Harleston Parker Gold Medal
of the Boston Society of Architects
and the City of Boston:
360 Newbury Street, Boston, MA
(with Frank O. Gehry & Associates, Design Architect).

1992
Honor Award,
Boston Society of Architects:
The Lazarus House, Copake, NY.

1991
Honor Award,
Boston Society of Architects:
Firehouse Arts Center,
Newburyport, MA.

1991
Honor Award,
Boston Society of Architects:
MIT Rotch Library of Art, Architecture and Planning,
Cambridge, MA.

1990
Honor Award,
Boston Society of Architects:
The Wheeler School Library,
Providence, RI.

1989
Honor Award,
Boston Society of Architects:
The Wellesley Fire Department Headquarters,
Wellesley, MA.

1987
Award for Excellence in Housing Design,
Boston Society of Architects:
The House at Tanglewood,
West Stockbridge, MA.

American Institute of Architects Regional Awards

1994
Merit Award,
New England Regional Council
of the American Institute of Architects:
Firehouse Arts Center, Newburyport, MA.

1993
Award for Excellence in Architecture,
New England Regional Council
of the American Institute of Architects:
The Lazarus House, Copake NY.

1991
Merit Award,
New England Regional Council
of the American Institute of Architects:
MIT Rotch Library of Art, Architecture and Planning,
Cambridge, MA.

1989
Merit Award,
California Regional Council of the
American Institute of Architects:
360 Newbury Street, Boston, MA
(with Frank O. Gehry & Associates, Design Architect).

1988
Award for Excellence in Architecture,
New England Regional Council
of the American Institute of Architects, Special Mention:
The House at Tanglewood,
West Stockbridge, MA.

1987
Award for Excellence in Architecture,
New England Regional Council
of the American Institute of Architects:
The Bellringers Bandshell,
Boston, MA.

Interior Design Awards

1990
Restaurants & Institutions
Interior Design Award:
The Coffee Connection, Boston, MA.

1990
IBD/Interior Design Award,
The Institute of Business Designers
and Interior Design Magazine:
The Spa at the Heritage, Boston, MA.

1990
First Place, International Store Interior
Design Competition, Institute of Store Planners
and National Retail Merchants Association:
Domain, Burlington, MA.

Specialty Awards

1999
Build Massachusetts Award,
Associated General Contractors
of Massachusetts, Merit Award:
The New England Aquarium
West Wing Addition, Boston, MA.

1995
Progessive Architecture Award,
Citation for Outstanding Design:
The Boston Children's Museum Addition
(with Frank O. Gehry & Associates, Design Architect).

1994
Wood Institute Award:
Proctor Academy Library & Learning Center,
Andover, NH.

1993
National Library Award,
American Institute of Architects
and the American Library Association:
MIT Rotch Library of Art, Architecture and Planning,
Cambridge, MA.

1991
Build Massachusetts Award,
Associated General Contractors
of Massachusetts, Merit Award:
MIT Rotch Library of Art, Architecture and Planning,
Cambridge, MA.

1991
Preservation Award,
The Boston Preservation Alliance:
Lobby at 50 Federal Street,
Boston, MA.

1990
Grand Award of the National Association of Industrial
and Office Parks/New England Chapter:
360 Newbury Street, Boston, MA
(with Frank O. Gehry & Associates, Design Architect).

1987
Build Massachusetts Award,
Associated General Contractors' Performance Award:
313 Congress Street, Boston, MA.

Employee History

Year of first employment
Current staff listed in **bold**

1980
Warren R. Schwartz, **Robert H. Silver** – founded Schwartz/Silver Architects Inc. on January 1st, 1980. Barbara Baluffi, K. Michael Hays, Martha Pilgreen, Harriet Balaran

1981
Mark Mahoney, Nader Tehrani, Michael Maltzan

1983
Ann Pitt, Kelly Wilson, James McQueen, Kathleen Lander Silver

1984
Mark Herman, Robert Miklos, Caroline Lander, Ann Marshall, Robert McLeod, Randi Gerson

1985
Paul Durand, Gia Daskalakis, Leo Chow, Ali Hocek, Gregory Zorzi, Jeff Klug, Rosa Perez, Claudia Deane, Thomas Goffigon, Joan Hallberg, Steven Lacker, Claudia Avidon, Andrea Homolac, Patrick LeClair, Dion McCarthy, Matthew Conley, Robin Donhoff, Christopher Kirwan, Mark Andonis Tsocanos,Ann Garrett, Brian Andrews, Laura Briggs, Paul Rovinelli

1986
David Stern, Mary Beth Gardner, Ann Katata, Mark Meche, Kenton Duckham, Robert Caddigan, Nancy Hackett, Thomas Fougere, **Nelson Liu**, Julie Fulton, Tobin Weaver, William Perry, Albert Ho, Celia Chiang, Karen Swett, Lisette Wong, Kathryn Blakeslee, Richard Rusch, Donna Mastroianni, Eric Schmidt, Donald Caddigan

1987
Kristin Rowe (Meche), **Randolph Meiklejohn**, Christopher Downey, Sara Laschever, Rania Matar Abouhamad, Satu Hirvonen, Damon Pride, **Christopher Ingersoll**

1989
June Thomas, Patrick Forrett, Michael Han, Timothy Downing, Elise Gispan, Barbara Frasier, Allison Saltzman

1990
Patricia Zoda, Elizabeth Taylor

1992
John Nakazawa, **Jonathan Traficonte**, Tiziano Fabrizio, Diane McCafferty, **Mark Schatz**, Mary Kate Riley, **Scott Peltier**

1994
Angela Ward Hyatt, Kathleen Lindstrom, Lisa Iwamoto, John Sheetz, Kyra Chomak, **Steven Gerrard**, Naomi Neville

1995
Mark McVay, **Philip Chen**, Patricia Anahory-Silva, **Peter Kleiner**, Sisia Daglian, Pamela Choi

1996
Kevin Plant, Kazuyo Oda, Nicole DeCongilio (Doran)

1997
Sandra Saccone, Anne Filson, Matthew Littell, Jonathan Kharfen, Amy Lin, Diana Wright-Boisrond, Christopher Chin, Karie Tseng, Christopher Keane, **Nick Dubrule**

1998
Scott Tulay, **Kathleen Monaghan**, Mimi Hoang, Sylvia Daniszewska

1999
Kristin Simonson, **Stephen Davis**, **Christopher Stanley**, **Amy Tangorra**, Wendy Cronk, Melissa Braisted, Brian Mulder, Henry Chang, Sam Silver, Francesco Brenta, **Michael Price**, Michelle Kim

2000
Ute Kupzog, **Michael Vinh**, **Michele Baldock**, **Jonathan Bolch**, **Susan Touloukian**, **Paul Stanbridge**, **Clair Colburn**